Writing for Canadian Health Professionals

SECOND EDITION

Lisa Salem-Wiseman

Humber College

Sobia Zaman

Humber College

TOP HAT   NELSON

TOP HAT

Writing for Canadian Health Professionals, Second Edition
by Lisa Salem-Wiseman and Sobia Zaman

Vice President, Editorial Higher Education:
Anne Williams

Executive Editor:
Laura Macleod

Executive Marketing Manager:
Amanda Henry

Developmental Editor:
Joanne Woods

Photo Researcher and Permissions Coordinator:
Sheila Hall

Senior Content Production Manager:
Natalia Denesiuk Harris

Production Service:
Cenveo Publisher Services

Copy Editor:
Lisa LaFramboise

Proofreader:
Pushpa

Indexer:
BIM Publishing Services

Design Director:
Ken Phipps

Managing Designer:
Franca Amore

Interior Design:
Peter Papayanakis

Cover Design:
Sharon Lucas

Cover Images:
RunPhoto/Getty Images (stethoscope); Charles Thatcher/Getty Images (hospital staff)

Library and Archives Canada Cataloguing in Publication Data

Salem-Wiseman, Lisa, author
    Writing for Canadian health professionals / Lisa Salem-Wiseman, Humber College, Sobia Zaman, Humber College. — Second edition.

Includes index.
ISBN 978-0-17-657222-8 (pbk.)

    1. Medical writing. I. Zaman, Sobia, author II. Title.

R119.S35 2014   808.06'661
C2013-907357-4

ISBN-13: 978-0-17-657222-8
ISBN-10: 0-17-657222-8

For Rachel and Jonathan. — L. S-W.

To my loved ones: past, present and future. — S.Z.

CONTENTS

The idea for *Writing for Canadian Health Professionals* grew out of several frustrating and fruitless searches for a writing textbook for our pre–health science students. We both teach writing courses aimed at students interested in becoming paramedics, nurses, funeral services workers, occupational therapist assistants, physiotherapist assistants, personal support workers, and pharmacy assistants. These are all fields in which poor written communication can have tragic consequences; therefore, it is essential that students in these programs learn to write accurately and effectively. Experience has taught us that these students learn communication skills best when their textbook incorporates health-related themes and content.

Unfortunately, although several colleges now offer courses specifically designed for students in the health sciences, there are very few writing textbooks designed specifically for the college and undergraduate health sciences student. We were looking for a textbook that (a) was Canadian, (b) was accessible to both the college and the university audience, (c) addressed the types of writing that students would be expected to produce in college and undergraduate university health sciences programs, (d) addressed the types of writing that graduates of these programs would be expected to produce in their workplaces, and (e) used examples from the real world of health care. When we were unable to find such a book, we decided to write one ourselves, and, judging by the success of the first edition, our instincts proved correct.

Writing for Canadian Health Professionals is the first of its kind in terms of student accessibility and Canadian content. It has been designed to help students in college and university health sciences programs as well as health professionals who wish to upgrade or review skills required to communicate effectively in writing. This book covers requisite communication skills for any Canadian health sciences student or health care professional in its presentation of the following key topics:

- relating the reasons why written communication is so vital in health care settings
- reviewing key grammar points and providing strategies to avoid and fix common errors
- conducting research using databases, search engines, and libraries
- documenting sources using APA format
- summarizing and analyzing written texts
- writing and formatting academic essays and reports
- writing effective resumés and cover letters
- communicating professionally by email
- writing narrative progress notes and structured progress notes

- understanding ethics and its importance in the health care workplace
- critically thinking about and expressing opinions on common and controversial health topics

In creating this text, we drew upon our experiences teaching writing to health sciences and pre–health sciences students, and we consulted colleagues, students, and health care professionals to ensure that the information and advice offered in this book is relevant, current, and practical.

NEW TO THIS EDITION

The following updates and additions have been made to the second edition of *Writing for Canadian Health Professionals*:

- content, exercises, and examples relevant to an even broader list of health care fields, including nursing, paramedics, physiotherapy, funeral services, and pharmacy
- an expanded section on commonly confused words
- updated examples and articles in all chapters
- an expanded section on conducting research
- a new chapter on incorporating and citing sources, including updated and expanded APA resources
- a new chapter on grammar that includes editing exercises
- a new chapter on teamwork and presentation skills
- new reflection and discussion activities
- additional anecdotes that express important and powerful health care realities
- a list of helpful websites at the end of each chapter
- changes to the short story and film selections

INSIDE THIS BOOK

All chapters include the following items:

- a list of **objectives**, so that students will clearly see what they can expect to have mastered by the end of the chapter
- a short **introduction**, explaining the relevance of the lessons to be covered
- **anecdotes** from health care professionals, chosen to illustrate the lessons in each chapter (indicated by the Anecdotes icon, featuring a photo of health care professionals, shown on page vii)
- "Try It Yourself" **exercises** to give students a chance to practise the new skills that they have learned (indicated by the Notebook icon, shown on page vii)
- a "Helpful Links" section at the end of each chapter that directs students to additional online resources (indicated by the chain link icon, shown on page vii)

Some chapters also include the following elements:

- an explanation of how students can use the **eight essential characteristics** of effective writing (outlined in Chapter Two) to achieve success in the types of writing covered in the chapter (indicated by the COCOACAT icon, featuring a cat, shown below). See page 18 for more on COCOACAT
- provocative **articles, stories, and poems** about important and controversial health issues (Canadian content is indicated by the maple leaf icon, shown below)
- opportunities for reflection that support a considered and compassionate connection to the material presented (indicated by the Reflections icon featuring a person deep in thought, shown below)
- **discussion** questions that allow students to discuss health-related concerns and controversies with their peers (indicated by the Discussion Activities icon featuring a photo of students working together, shown below)
- **examples** from student assignments and/or professional documents

Chapter One explains why good writing is essential in health care and demonstrates the impact that poor documentation can have on the lives affected.

Chapter Two provides a list of eight essential characteristics of effective writing for those involved in health care. This chapter also reviews essential grammar points and provides strategies for fixing common grammar errors.

Chapter Three introduces students to common types of documents that they will be expected to produce in academic health sciences programs.

Chapter Four takes students through the process of finding sources for their academic writing, outlines the research process, discusses the ethics and consequences of plagiarism, and shows them how to correctly cite sources according to APA standards.

Chapter Five introduces students to common documents that they will be expected to produce in a professional context, both in their efforts to seek employment in the allied health field, and in their working lives as health care professionals.

Chapter Six defines ethics, explores some of the ethical situations that health sciences students and health professionals might face, and provides excerpts from the codes of ethics for various professional organizations.

Chapter Seven discusses the skills involved in working in teams and developing and delivering effective presentations. These essential communication skills will contribute to students' academic and professional success.

Chapter Eight encourages students to reflect upon and write about important health issues and themes by exploring provocative health-related fiction and film.

We are both very excited by the second edition of *Writing for Canadian Health Professionals,* particularly at the prospect of using a text that is even more comprehensive than the first, yet still incorporates the successes of the first edition in being accessible, practical, and informative. As much of the book's new content has already been "class-tested," we are confident that this resource will help you achieve your goals, both inside and outside of the classroom.

Happy teaching and learning!

Lisa Salem-Wiseman and Sobia Zaman

ACKNOWLEDGMENTS

The idea for this book was conceived while we were both teaching writing to pre-health students in Humber's General Arts and Science program, so the first and most important thanks go to our students, who encouraged us to write this book and who have been generous with their input and feedback over the last few years. Specific mention goes to contributors Erlinda Taruc, Deejay Gonzales, Winter Hill, Rachel Orsini, Mari Flores, and Selina Tang. Gratitude is also due to our colleagues at Humber for their encouragement and enthusiasm—special thanks go to Tanya D'Anger, Judy Clarke, Franc Jamieson, Colin Macrae, Suzanne Moore, Patricia Morgan, Wendy Phillips, Mary Takacs, and the Humber College Career Centre.

Thanks also go to the Nelson Education higher education team for their dedication and effort: Laura Macleod, Joanne Woods, Natalia Denesiuk Harris, Ann Byford, Amanda Henry, Franca Amore, Sheila Hall, and Lisa LaFramboise.

We also greatly benefited from the feedback offered by those who reviewed this book, including Mark Feltham, Fanshawe College; Shannon MacRae, Niagara College; Suzanne Moore, Humber College; and Jennifer Timer, Langara College.

On a personal note, Lisa would like to acknowledge the support and patience of Jonathan and Rachel, as well as the encouragement and expertise of her parents, both of whom have had successful careers as health professionals, and both of whom are excellent writers. She also thanks her students, from whom she continues to learn year after year.

Sobia would like to thank all the lovely individuals in her life who never lost patience with her for being too busy "working on the book." As well, she would like to acknowledge those former students who have gone on to successful health sciences careers, confirming the role that a good communications text plays in that success. It is her hope that current and future students will continue to benefit from the knowledge contained herein.

WRITING AS ESSENTIAL IN HEALTH CARE: REASONS AND CONSEQUENCES

CHAPTER OBJECTIVES | *At the end of this chapter, you should be able to*

- understand why good writing skills are essential for a health sciences career
- comprehend the magnitude of consequences that can result from poor writing and negligent documentation in a health care environment
- analyze and discuss real-life case studies that demonstrate the serious consequences of documentation lapses in health care

INTRODUCTION

More often than not, students interested in a health sciences career are disappointed when they see writing courses on their program timetables. College and university writing professors often hear the following responses from their students: "I know how to write!"; "I don't need a writing course!"; "What does grammar have to do with saving lives?"; "This is a waste of time!" Often, the student interested in paramedics just wants to "jump in" and start saving lives as opposed to attending to any deficiencies in spelling or grammar. Similarly, the nursing student becomes focused on studying blood pressure and medication administration, while the physiotherapy student might be more excited by the prospect of learning physical manipulation techniques than by learning how to write clearly and concisely. Such common responses to English courses in the health care stream clearly demonstrate a lack of awareness about the important role writing plays in that field.

As you go through this chapter, you will discover eight reasons why postsecondary health sciences programs make every effort to ensure that their graduates have good writing skills. While health sciences students may not find writing courses as "sexy" as anatomy or psychology, this chapter outlines why these courses should be taken seriously and illustrates how they can have a tremendous impact, both academically and professionally.

This chapter begins by outlining eight reasons why writing in health care is an essential skill, and then presents, for discussion and analysis, real-life case scenarios that demonstrate the consequences of negligent writing or record-keeping in health care.

EIGHT REASONS WHY WRITING IN THE HEALTH SCIENCES IS AN ESSENTIAL SKILL

Writing is a crucial skill in most professions and even more so in the busy and challenging environment of health care because of its potential impact on the physical and mental well-being of individuals. If you are planning to enter a health care field, what follows are eight good reasons why you must be able to write properly.

1) Your College or University Program Requires It

Unfortunately, success in a health care field cannot come without first meeting the academic demands of a postsecondary institution. Success in most academic programs depends on a student's ability to communicate his or her thoughts effectively. Whether an individual is pursuing a four-year university degree or a two-year college diploma, he or she must demonstrate some degree of writing proficiency in order to be successful in his or her academic training. In a Bachelor of Nursing program, for example, students are expected to show competence in various types of document writing, including research reports, literature reviews, health promotion assignments, progress reports, and field reports. A student's inability to handle the writing demands of such tasks can lead to failure.

In addition to program-specific writing, health sciences students may find themselves in a position of having to take extra writing courses in order to upgrade their current skill level. These extra courses can vary greatly in content; some teach basic grammar concepts, while others offer practice with more complex and lengthier prose. Many postsecondary programs also require that health sciences students take electives or general education courses, many of which may be writing intensive.

It is also important to note that on the path to a rewarding health science career, a well-written, well-structured resumé and cover letter are essential. Individuals interested in working in the field of health sciences must, then, continue to demonstrate well-honed writing skills in order to effectively market themselves as competent professionals worthy of being hired.

2) The Writing Process Mirrors Essential Workplace Skills

Good writing, like most things, is a process that takes concerted effort. It requires knowledge, organization and logic, as well as the ability to think critically and make sound decisions. As you work to improve your writing skills, you are, in fact, practising and reinforcing the very skills that are essential when working in health care.

In order to write competently and effectively, you first need to understand the foundation of good writing. This means grasping grammar fundamentals and knowing how best to organize the information you wish to convey. Such attention to detail and organization is crucial as documentation in health care facilities supports a logical flow of information, both in the way that forms and charts are structured and in the way they are meant to be used. Additionally, common chart formats, like SOAP (see Chapter 4), require health care workers to methodically assess clients in a prescribed and logical way.

Good writers are also often strong critical thinkers. They know what constitutes sloppy thinking and work hard to avoid constructions that are lazy or simplistic lest their writing undermine their professional or academic credibility. The critical thinking reinforced by the academic writing process translates effectively into the health care workplace where the ability of health practitioners to recognize patterns, at the core of much critical thinking, is required in many situations including in the interpretation of symptoms. Critical thinking is, in fact, a pervasive requirement in health care. Nurses, for example, regularly assess whether a treatment is working or not and must be able to handle unexpected deterioration of those in their care. Paramedics also rely on critical thinking. They need to consider the quickest route to a location, address the diversity of casualties they encounter on a call, and, in the case of mass casualties, strategize as to the order of victim response. Similarly, funeral services workers use critical thinking when advising clients. They have to find ways to support a client's vision of a loved one's service whether that entails requests for the unusual or the non-traditional, or modifications based on religious beliefs.

Good writers are also constantly engaged in the decision-making process, having to make decisions on word choice, tone, and level of language. Mostly, they have to be adept at selection of content, filtering information in such a way that they communicate the most salient points of their intended message. In the health care workplace, patients and their family members, all in varying degrees of distress, bombard health professionals with a myriad of confused, disordered, random, and sometimes contradictory information, and the health care worker must be able to retrieve the most pertinent and relevant content in order to provide proper and expedient care. Health is a complex matter; medical histories can be vast, and people in distress rely on front-line workers to articulate and prescribe their needs into the language of effective care.

So working in a health care environment requires knowledge, logic, organization, critical thinking, and sound decision-making skills, the very skills reinforced by the writing process. The importance of these skills is corroborated by Human Resources and Skills Development Canada, which ranks problem solving, decision making, and critical thinking as top skills in several health care professions (see Table 1.1).

TABLE 1.1	**Essential Skills in Health Care Professions**
PROFESSION	**ESSENTIAL SKILLS**
REGISTERED NURSE	Document Use Oral Communication Problem Solving
PRACTICAL NURSE	Oral Communication Decision Making
PARAMEDIC	Document Use Oral Communication Problem Solving
FUNERAL DIRECTORS AND EMBALMERS	Document Use Oral Communication Job task planning and organizing
PHARMACIST	Oral Communication Critical Thinking

Source: Adapted from tables in "Essential skills profiles: Explore careers by skills and knowledge." Literacy and Essential Skills, Human Resources and Skills Development Canada (http://www.hrsdc.gc.ca).

3) Your Job Demands It

People are attracted to a career in the health sciences for a multitude of reasons, which may include a desire to help others, personal or familial experience with illness, or a desire to have a career as exciting as those portrayed in television dramas such as *Grey's Anatomy* and *House*. Individuals lured into a health sciences career by the appeal and marketing of hospital-centred television dramas must, however, consider one of the least dramatic aspects of the job: the time spent on written documentation.

In addition to rounds and other responsibilities, nurses are required to complete assessment and progress notes and construct detailed patient care plans, as are many other health care providers. Health care professionals may also write research reports and educational materials, as well as contributing to professional journals.

Recently, an American study chronicled the division of time nurses spent on certain duties during a shift, concluding that mostof a nurse's time was consumed by some form of documentation work. In this study, the breakdown of tasks by percentage reveals the significant amount of time spent on written tasks in nursing: documentation 35.3%; care coordination 20.6%; medication administration 17.2%; patient care activities 19.3%; patient assessment and interpretation of vital signs 7.2% (Hendrich, Chow, Skierczynski, & Zhenqiang, 2008).

As shown in Table 1.1, document use has also been highlighted as a high priority skill in health care by Human Resources and Skills Development Canada. Strong writing skills are also listed as a requisite skill in most job postings related to heath care.

While many forms in health care facilities are designed to be user-friendly and efficient in their incorporation of checklists and flow charts, it is important to note that these documents are used in varying degrees at different institutions.

4) Communication Errors in the Workplace Translate into Incompetence

The Health Council of Canada, in its 2006 Annual Report, alluded to the role that poor penmanship and rushed data entry can play in sacrificing quality patient care: "The health of Canadians is being compromised by illegible handwriting and errors in the manual entry and processing of drug prescriptions" (p. 69). Despite the incorporation of computerized information management systems in many Canadian medical facilities, there are still some tasks that require handwriting, so neatnesss and legibility are paramount. This same report emphasizes that documentation systems in Canadian hospitals are in need of improvement in terms of efficiency, reliability, and accuracy (pp. 64–65).

Documentation errors in a medical facility occur for many different reasons and, ultimately, point to areas in need of improvement and change. In Canadian hospitals, inefficient documentation systems, lack of time to document comprehensively, the distractions of multi-tasking, and lack of proper education in the principles of professional written communication are often cited by health care workers as factors that inhibit their ability to handle important documentation-related tasks successfully.

5) Others Look at What You Write

As in most occupations, health care professionals do not work independently; they are expected to work as members of a cooperative, effective, and efficient team. A patient in a hospital will likely have numerous attendants over the course of a hospital stay. In other words, there is more than one recorder of information, as well as more than one reader of information. As all members of the health care team rely on the same notes for guidance, assessment, and treatment purposes, clarity and accuracy become the responsibility of each and every caregiver if quality patient care is to be maintained. In a busy medical practice or hospital environment, it is clearly not feasible to hunt down previous caregivers for the purpose of seeking clarification on notes that should have been entered comprehensively and accurately in the first place. Rather, all documentation must be complete and precise at the time of recording so the patient will be treated effectively and efficiently by each and every member of the health care team that aids in his or her well-being.

6) Writing Well Protects You

If a patient dies under unusual circumstances or has unexpected complications, patient documentation becomes a key piece of evidence in determining the nature of complication or death, as well as in constructing a reliable timeline in the event of a medical or criminal investigation. For the purposes of protection from accusations of wrongdoing, proper and accurate documentation is crucial; without comprehensive documentation, health care professionals set themselves, and their institutions, up for malpractice suits. Such suits drain time, energy, and resources of all involved and often end up damaging individual and institutional reputations.

In the sensitive area of health, individuals and families demand professional, honest, and reliable care from those trained to aid them. It is, for example, not uncommon for patients to attempt to sue health care practitioners or their institutions if they believe that their loved one was not treated or dealt with professionally, competently, or ethically. Indeed, such cases appear to be happening more frequently given the number of health-related malpractice suits.

One way in which health care providers can help protect themselves from false accusations and unreasonable malpractice suits is to ensure that anything they document is accurate and comprehensive. Written documentation is an important piece of evidence in the courtroom, where the spoken word has little weight in comparison to professional and detailed notes that effectively substantiate that an accused nurse or paramedic was not negligent. If there was no witness present at the time of an alleged incident with a patient, the written record of engagement with the patient is the only evidence chronicling the events leading up to an incident, complication, or death. Courts are impressed by accurate and complete notes, so health care practitioners must protect themselves and their institutions by leaving a trail of accurate and concise documentation. Additionally, the judicial process can be slow and tedious; archived medical records can be pulled up to be examined by coroners, police officers, and lawyers years after an incident. Human memory erodes over time, so legible, accurate, and comprehensive notes must compensate.

I've been a nurse for a long time and remember attending a professional development session, eons ago, where they showed a video clip of a lawyer questioning a nurse in some kind of malpractice case. The lawyer was ruthless! He had samples of the nurse's charting and blew it up on a HUGE screen so that the judge and jury could see the errors it contained. The nurse didn't stand a chance; what defence is there for sloppy documentation? Her charts were almost illegible, with words scratched out. She also misused some standardized symbols. Even though I'm a nurse, I did not feel sorry for the woman on the videotape. If she looked incompetent and unprofessional, she brought that upon herself. The whole situation reminded me of how much our written documentation affects our reputation and credibility. This is serious stuff.

—RPN (hospital)

"It's been devastating for the institution. The people involved are terribly upset. We feel terribly for the loss the family has suffered. We offered our profound apologies. Claire's death could have been avoided," he said.

Paul Harte, the Lewis family's lawyer, said he believes the apology is the result of both his clients' badgering and a changing health-care culture. More amazing, he says, is that the family received an apology at all.

"All I do is sue doctors and nurses," said Harte, who has been a medical malpractice specialist for almost nine years. "I've never had occasion to see a hospital admit liability. The hospital should be lauded for admitting responsibility."

Lawyers for Hamilton Health Sciences and the Lewis family are close to reaching a settlement.

Sitting by the Christmas tree, the heavy scent of cooked vegetables and incense in the air, John Lewis acknowledged that his family may seem composed on the surface.

The reality is that the Lewis family's pain is excruciatingly potent 14 months after Claire's death. John says no one can understand the depth and power of their grief but those who have experienced the loss of a child themselves.

"We get out of bed in the morning, put a foot in front of the other, keep breathing and get through the day. Not a day goes by that there's not tears in this house."

He retells the story of Claire's death and the hospital's response with a simmering fury. Short breaks and deep breaths are necessary to keep from boiling over.

"Not one of (the staff members whose errors claimed Claire's life) has stepped forward and said, I am responsible and accountable for this. I want an acknowledgement of my child's life and my child's death and of my pain and suffering. I want them to look at me and say, 'I'm sorry sir, it will never happen again.'"

Source: From "A grief without end: Hospital apologizes to 11-year-old's family for the errors that killed her,"
by Jocelyn Bell, 2002, Dec. 26, The Hamilton Spectator, *p. A1. Used with permission from* The Hamilton Spectator,
http://www.thespec.com. Copyright The Hamilton Spectator. All rights reserved.

Discussion Questions:

1. What happened to Claire Lewis?

2. What factors led up to Claire's death?

3. What role did poor documentation or poor record-keeping play in Claire's death?

4. Could Claire's death have been prevented? If so, how?

5. How did the hospital respond to the situation?

6. How did the family respond to the situation?

7. Why is the family's lawyer surprised by the hospital's apology?

8. Does the family accept the hospital's apology? Why or why not?

9. Does anything in this story shock or surprise you?

10. What does this case teach us about documentation in health care?

BOX 1.3	**Case Study: Medication Administration Error and Failure to Monitor**
	Settlement: $100,000 **Legal Expenses:** $6,152

Note: There were multiple co-defendants in this claim who are not discussed in this scenario. While there may have been errors/negligent acts on the part of other defendants, the case, comments and recommendations are limited to the actions of the defendant: the intensive care nurse.

A 23-year-old woman with no significant medical history presented to the emergency room with flu-like symptoms. She complained of generalized body ache and had a fever of 102.6. For the past two weeks, she had self-administered over-the-counter medications with no relief. Instead, her condition deteriorated and she developed both shortness of breath and a cough. Her worsening symptoms motivated her to seek care at a local emergency room.

Following an abnormal CT Scan of the chest (near-complete collapse of right upper lobe, large consolidation of the right lower lobe, and moderate consolidation of the left lower lobe of the lungs), and elevated white blood count (19,500), abnormal liver function tests and an abnormal coagulation profile, the emergency department physician admitted the patient to the intensive care unit under the care of an attending physician. The patient was started on oxygen and antibiotic therapy. Blood cultures were drawn and showed Streptococcus Pneumoniae, and antibiotics were appropriately adjusted per recommendation of the infectious disease specialist.

The attending physician first saw the patient in the intensive care unit. At the time of his initial exam, the patient was not in significant respiratory distress, was responding well to the oxygen and antibiotic therapy, and was subsequently continued on the same therapy. The attending physician noted that while the patient was not in acute distress, her blood chemistry was abnormal with a potassium level of 2.9 (normal range is 3.5 to 5.0). The physician ordered 30 mEq of potassium to be added to each bag of the patient's intravenous fluid, infused at 80 milliliters per hour. The order was to be maintained through the remainder of her course of treatment.

Two days later and despite the potassium added to her intravenous fluids, the patient's potassium level was noted to be 3.0 and the attending physician ordered 80 mEq of potassium to be administered by mouth. The patient vomited the medication (amount retained undetermined). The attending physician then ordered two doses of 40 mEq of intravenous potassium to infuse over a four hour time period with the plan of increasing the potassium level between 4 and 4.5. Documentation is problematic. It appears that despite the order for two doses of potassium 40 mEq to be infused over four hours, the intensive care unit nurse administered two intravenous potassium doses of 20 mEq over approximately one hour (documentation regarding this is inconclusive).

Throughout the day the intensive care unit nurse documented the patient's heart rate in the patient care record. At 7:30 a.m. it was 72 beats per minute, at 1:30 p.m. it was 96 beats per minute and at 4:30 p.m. it was 116 beats per minute. The patient's blood pressure remained stable at 120/80. The intensive care unit nurse did not specifically notify the physician of the pattern of rising heart rate. When the physician saw the patient that day, he noted that the patient's white blood cell and platelet counts remained higher than normal but were dropping. In addition, her vital signs were within normal range and she was not in respiratory distress. He ordered a pulmonary consult for possible bronchoscopy but deemed that she was stable, and that the vasopressors and aggressive pulmonary treatment were not necessary at that time. He ordered the patient to be transferred to the telemetry unit.

The intensive care nurse's documentation fails to provide the exact time of transfer from the intensive care unit to the telemetry unit although it appears to have been between 7:15 p.m. and 7:30 p.m. The documentation also fails to validate the intensive care nurse's statement that the patient was on a cardiac monitor during her intensive care stay and that she was transferred to the telemetry unit with a cardiac monitor and oxygen therapy. The telemetry unit nurse stated the patient did not arrive with a monitor. Other telemetry staff indicated that the telemetry unit was in an overflow situation when the patient

continued

was transferred and the central monitoring station was not functioning. Regardless of the actual reason, there are no telemetry unit electrocardiogram strips for this patient.

According to the hospital records, the attending physician was called at approximately 10:00 p.m. and was advised that the patient had gone into cardiac arrest. The on-call emergency physician attempted to resuscitate, but was unable to obtain a heart beat and the patient was pronounced dead.

The family of the deceased sued the attending physician, the hospital and three of the hospital's registered nurses, and sought $3,000,000 in damages. The allegations against the intensive care unit nurse included alleged failure to properly administer the medications as ordered by the physician and failure to notify the attending physician of significant changes in the patient's vital signs and laboratory results.

Initially, the defense team felt the intensive care unit nurse had a strong case. She stated she had done nothing wrong. She indicated that she did not believe that she had enough experience and should not have been working in the intensive care unit. Despite her limited clinical skills, she believed she followed the physician's orders appropriately and documented her actions thoroughly. She recalled administering the potassium and believed she had advised the physician when necessary. She further believed she had properly documented her actions throughout her care to the patient.

When an expert witness examined the case, he noted that the intensive care unit nurse administered an incorrect dosage of medication over a shorter period of time. The expert also noted that nursing protocols required that the discharging intensive care unit nurse should have specifically noted the time of transfer, the patient's condition at the time, the patient's current treatment, the patient's response to treatment and the specific equipment transported with the patient. Documentation of these items is inadequate or missing. The intensive care unit nurse's notes suggested that the patient's heart rate had increased at an alarming rate that day and this should have resulted in the nurse calling the attending physician to assess the impact if the patient's rising pulse on the transfer and medication orders.

Resolution

After the expert witness stated that the intensive care unit nurse's care and treatment of the patient was not medically defensible, the claim against her settled at mediation for $100,000 with an additional $6,152 in legal expenses. The total settlement amongst all of the defendants in the case was $1.4 million.

Source: "Case study: Medication administration error and failure to monitor," by Nurses Service Organization and CNA Financial Corporation, 2010, Nurses and Medical Malpractice: Case Study with Risk Management Strategies, Chicago: Continental Casualty Company; New York: Affinity Insurance Services. Retrieved from https://www.nso.com/pdfs/db/Nurse_SLCS_x-8540-510_final_web.pdf?fileName=Nurse_SLCS_x-8540-510_final_web.pdf&folder=pdfs/db&isLiveStr=Y. Reprinted with permission from Nurses Service Organization (NSO); 159 E. County Line Road, Hatboro, PA 19040, 1-800-247-1500. Case Study: Medication Administration Error and Failure to Monitor.

Discussion Questions:

1. The case study above includes medical terminology you might not be familiar with. Define the following words and phrases: CT Scan, coagulation, Streptococcus Pneumoniae, intravenous, infused, mEq, white blood cell, platelet, vital signs, pulmonary, bronchoscopy, vasopressors, telemetry, electrocardiogram, cardiac arrest.

2. What symptoms did the 23-year-old woman have when she first presented to the emergency room?

3. Why was she admitted to the intensive care unit?

4. Summarize her experiences once she was admitted to the intensive care unit.

5. Find examples of inadequate, inconclusive, and absent documentation as it pertains to her treatment in the intensive care unit.

6. Do you think that negligent documentation played a role in the patient's death?

7. What does this case suggest about human memory versus comprehensive documentation in health care?

8. What criminal allegations did the family lay against the hospital and the health care team (physician, nurses) responsible for their loved one's care?

9. How did the intensive care nurse defend her actions? Do you find her defense valid? Why or why not?

10. Based on the events as reported, who do you believe to be most at fault in this scenario?

11. Do you think the patient's death could have been prevented? If so, how?

12. What did the expert witness conclude?

13. Why do you think that individuals sue in such matters? Do you think that money can compensate for the loss of a loved one? In this specific case, do you think the financial compensation awarded to the family was just?

CHAPTER LINKS FOR FURTHER EXPLORATION

- **Canadian Paramedicine (http://www.emsnews.com)**

This site contains resource material on paramedicine and may be of interest to current paramedics or those interested in working in the field. It features news articles relevant to paramedics and health care, and provides multiple choice quizzes that test understanding of a variety of paramedic scenarios.

- **College of Registered Nurses of British Columbia (https://www.crnbc.ca)**

Many items related to nursing, including an overview of the profession, the standards for nursing practice, and an explanation of the different nursing designations are presented here. In the site's *Practice Standards* section, the importance of documentation and the rules that need to be followed corroborate the information presented in this chapter. Case studies on various nursing scenarios are also included.

- **Employment and Social Development Canada (http://www.hrsdc.gc.ca)**

This government website is a good source of information for those interested in health care work. It informs readers about essential health care skills, student financial assistance, and labour market trends.

REFERENCE

Hendrich, A., Chow, M. P., Skierczynski, B. A., & Zhenqiang, L. (2008). A 36-hospital time and motion study: How do medical-surgical nurses spend their time? *The Permanente Journal 12*(3), 25–34. Retrieved from http://www.ncbi.nlm.nih.gov/pmc/articles/PMC3037121

WRITING FOR SUCCESS: TRAITS, GRAMMAR, AND EDITING

At the end of this chapter, you should be able to

- understand and apply the eight essential characteristics of effective writing in the health sciences
- review grammar rules in the areas of subject–verb agreement, pronoun choices, sentence errors, modifiers, and punctuation.
- skillfully proofread documents in order to determine errors in grammar and effective writing
- edit and revise your writing to reflect proper grammar and the eight essential characteristics of effective writing

INTRODUCTION

As highlighted in the previous chapter, being a competent writer is important, both in your college or university health sciences program and in the workplace. To help you prepare for the writing expectations you will encounter in both places, in this chapter we look closely at exactly what writing well in health care means and provide you with guidance on how to achieve this standard. We also review writing fundamentals in key grammar areas like subject–verb agreement, pronoun choices, sentence errors, modifiers, and punctuation, in order that you learn to recognize and eliminate errors created by incorrect usage. Once you understand the basic rules of grammar, you will see a noticeable improvement in your writing and feel more confident as you edit and revise your documents to meet professional and academic standards.

Before we look at the specific writing traits that are important in the health sciences, take a few minutes to reflect on your current understanding of what writing well means. What does it mean to write well? How might writing in the health sciences differ from writing in other fields like the creative arts or marketing? Are there any similarities between writing in the different disciplines? Write a thoughtful response that considers these questions. Your instructor may ask you to share your reflection with the class.

WRITING TRAITS FOR THE HEALTH SCIENCES

In Chapter 1, we established why writing well is important to the health professions. This section will focus on what exactly writing well means in the health context.

Every academic discipline has its own set of expectations for good writing, and the health sciences are no different. The elegant, imaginative, expressive style of writing that earned you an A in your high school or college literature class will not earn you the same mark in NRS 101: Nursing as a Profession or PSYC 121: Applied Psychology 1. You will be expected to produce assignments that are **clear, objective, concise, organized, accurate, correct, audience-appropriate,** and **thorough.**

Furthermore, once you graduate and are working in the health care industry, you will be expected to communicate in a clear, objective, concise, organized, accurate, correct, audience-appropriate, and thorough manner ... and all while under extreme pressure in a fast-paced, stressful environment that is full of distractions!

Because health care workers often work in shifts, their coworkers need to be able to pick up their notes and understand exactly what is going on with a patient. Effective documentation is crucial to good patient care.

In order to help you become an effective communicator, we will introduce you to the eight qualities of health care communication that have been consistently identified as most important by qualified health care professionals. Whether you are writing a lab report for chemistry class, a research report on the Canadian health care system, an incident report, or notes on a patient's chart, these eight principles will help ensure that your communication is effective. The acronym COCOACAT can help you remember some important traits about health sciences writing.

COCOA CAT

C   clear
O   objective
C   concise
O   organized
A   accurate
C   correct
A   audience-appropriate
T   thorough

C is for CLEAR

A common complaint of many health professionals is that much of the written communication they see in the workplace is unclear or vague and contains confusing wording.

Communication in the world of health care needs to be clear and unambiguous for the following reasons:

- Many health care workplaces are collaborative environments; therefore, others should be able to pick up a health care worker's notes and understand exactly what is going on with a patient.
- A misunderstood instruction can lead to serious or even fatal consequences.
- Documentation can be subpoenaed, so each piece needs to be able to stand on its own as a legal record.

Tips for Improving Clarity

1. When given a choice between a familiar term and an obscure term, the more familiar term is preferable, as long as the meaning stays the same. When writing for a general audience, define any technical terms that are specific to your profession.

2. Read over what you have written, asking yourself whether your intended meaning is obvious to the reader.

TRY IT YOURSELF

What meaning do you think was intended in each of the following statements taken from real life examples of nurses' writing? Try to determine exactly where and why each statement is unclear. Using the space provided, correct each sentence to make its meaning clearer.

1. "Patient is awake and alert with many visitors in bed."

2. "Patient may shower with assistants."

3. "The resident came in from the garden and threw a dog at the television."

4. "Patient became ill after eating too many turtles while at the zoo."

5. "The nurse delivered the baby, cut and clamped the cord, and handed it to the paediatrician."

Source: Courtesy of Doctors Lounge, http://www.doctorslounge.com

O is for OBJECTIVE

Scientific writing must be objective, that is, free of personal assumptions, biases, feelings, or opinions. There are a few reasons for this:

- Results of tests or experiments will only be considered valid if another professional would be able to produce the same results. Therefore, the focus is on the work, not the worker.
- Notes and charts can be made public; therefore, judgments such as "the patient was whining," "the wound is giving off a disgusting odour," or "this patient is a nightmare" are inappropriate.
- Personal impressions are subjective, that is, dependent on a person's moods, opinions, attitudes, and beliefs. Such impressions communicate very little real information. If a person is described as "old," is he or she 45? 60? 95? Is a "hot" day 20 degrees Celsius? 30? 40?

Tips for Achieving an Objective Tone

1. Avoid starting sentences with "I" or "we": this pulls focus away from the scientific topic at hand.

2. Avoid using "I think" or "we believe." Everything you say should follow from logic, not from personal bias or subjectivity. Never use emotive words (such as feel, believe, or think) or words that imply judgment (such as seems, appears, or looks like).

3. Stick to what can be observed; don't "fill in the blanks" by making assumptions. If a patient stumbles when walking into a clinic and appears disoriented and confused while giving her history, do not record that "the patient was drunk." Record the behaviour, but don't guess at the cause, even if it seems to be obvious.

4. Avoid making judgments based on data. Record the data; don't interpret it.

TRY IT YOURSELF

Here are a student's observations of an experiment in which a mouse in a maze was given two pathways to choose from, only one of which led to food. Underline all the SUBJECTIVE elements in this paragraph. Now, rewrite it as an OBJECTIVE, facts-only scientific description.

The little grey mouse carefully peered down each pathway. Finally, after thinking about it for a while, it decided to venture down the path on the right. The mouse started tentatively down that pathway, but it stopped, confused, when it failed to find any food. It turned around and went back to the start. I think the mouse must have been hungry, because it rushed down the pathway on the left and greedily gobbled up all of its food.

C is for CONCISE

Health care professionals have to convey large amounts of information quickly, and in small spaces on forms and charts. It is important to be direct, avoid repetition and irrelevant information, and summarize data whenever possible.

Tips for Making Writing Concise

1. Avoid wordy phrases:

   a) "at this point in time" can be reworded as "now"
   b) "at a later date" can be reworded as "later"

2. Cut meaningless words or phrases that add no meaning:

   c) "all things considered"
   d) "for all intents and purposes"
   e) "as far as I'm concerned"
   f) "in my opinion"

3. Avoid redundant or repetitive phrases:

   g) "8 a.m. in the morning" can be changed to "8 a.m."
   h) "fewer in number" can be changed to "fewer"

4. Combine sentences to reduce length:

   i) Janet is studying. She is tired. She is preparing for her anatomy exam. It is her last exam.
   j) Although Janet is tired, she is studying for her last exam, which is anatomy.

TRY IT YOURSELF

Rewrite the following sentences to eliminate repetition, irrelevant information, and empty words and phrases.

1. The accident occurred at 2 p.m. in the afternoon.

2. In this day and age, nursing is a popular career choice for men as well as women.

3. Eva's little brother was eating popcorn. A piece became stuck in his throat. He couldn't breathe. He was turning blue. Eva performed the Heimlich manoeuvre. The popcorn flew across the room. He gasped, coughed, and began breathing normally.

4. In the clinic, staff attend to critically ill patients who are very sick.

5. Due to the fact that the flu can be fatal, it is important for people 65 years of age or older to have a flu shot.

O is for ORGANIZED

For communication in the health professions to be effective, it needs to be organized in a logical manner that makes it easy to understand.

Tips for Improving Organization

1. State your main point clearly and near the beginning of your piece of writing.

2. Put the most important information first.

3. Make a statement or claim first, and then back it up with any details or examples.

4. When relating an incident, describe the events in the order in which they occurred (chronological order).

5. Use transitional words (*first, next, finally, after, therefore*) and phrases (*as a result, before beginning*) to connect ideas.

6. Use cues such as headings, topic sentences, transition words, lists, and graphics.

TRY IT YOURSELF

Rearrange the sentences in the following paragraph in a more logical order, adding transitional words and phrases when needed. You may combine sentences and/or omit words.

> *Dr. James Young, at St. Jude's hospital, examined me and told me that my left shoulder was dislocated. At 9:00 a.m. that morning, the store manager, Rose Daniels, asked me to hang a large plastic skeleton over the customer service desk. When I got to work that morning she had asked me to get the ladder from the storeroom. I leaned too far to the left and lost my balance. I climbed to the top rung and attempted to hang the skeleton, but I couldn't reach the hook on the ceiling. I landed on my left shoulder and couldn't move. I screamed in pain and Ms. Daniels called the paramedics. On Tuesday, October 23, I was injured when I fell off a ladder while hanging Halloween decorations in my workplace, David's Books.*

A is for ACCURATE

Accuracy is extremely important in scientific writing. An accurate description of the location of pain or the size of a wound or the amount of a substance to be administered could be vital.

Tips for Improving Accuracy

1. Pay attention to word choice and make sure that you are using the correct word. Know the terminology associated with the subject.

2. Include all essential information, including measurements and quantities.

3. Use proper names for people, places, and medications.

4. Avoid vague terms like "good" and "worse" and qualifiers such as "very" or "really." Give specific information.

TRY IT YOURSELF

What essential information is missing from the following paragraph? Edit the paragraph to make it more accurate. You will need to be creative and make up details.

> *Angela Jones arrived at the clinic early in the morning with her baby daughter, Maria. The child had a high fever and a bad cough. Ms. Jones told the receptionist that Maria had started coughing a few days ago and that the cough had gotten worse. After some time in the waiting room, Maria was taken to see a doctor, who prescribed some medicine.*

C is for CORRECT

The first question that students ask upon receiving an assignment is often "Does spelling count?" The answer should always be "Yes." One problem frequently cited by nurse managers, doctors, and other health professionals is basic errors in spelling, punctuation, and grammar. Such errors reflect poorly upon the writer, and are often assumed to be a sign of a more general carelessness or lack of attention to detail; in the health professions, such carelessness can—quite literally—be fatal. Misspelled drug names, misplaced decimals, grammatical errors, or misused words could have serious consequences.

Tips for Correcting Errors

If you are writing on a computer, use the spell-check software, but do not rely on it too much. In addition, try the following:

1. Use a dictionary when you write.

2. Familiarize yourself with commonly confused words.

3. Proofread everything you have written.

4. Use correct grammar. Your word processor's grammar checker can help you to identify errors, but you should keep a grammar handbook nearby to ensure that you know how to correct them.

5. Read carefully, thinking about the logic of what you have written.

Check and double-check the spelling of all proper nouns, including people's names, locations, addresses, procedures, equipment, and medications. Some **commonly confused words** include the following:

- ACCEPT: to receive
  EXCEPT: to take or leave out; excluding

  I will <u>accept</u> all the applications <u>except</u> for yours.

- ADVISE: to counsel or direct (verb)
  ADVICE: guidance (noun)

  The nurse <u>advised</u> her patient to walk slowly after the surgery; fortunately, the patient followed her <u>advice</u> and did not injure herself.

- AFFECT: to influence (verb)
  EFFECT: a result (noun)

  The <u>effect</u> of sun exposure is premature aging of the skin.

  Too much exposure to sun has <u>affected</u> her appearance.

- A LOT: many
  ALOT: no such word

  We saw <u>a lot</u> of patients this morning.

- ALL RIGHT: satisfactory
  ALRIGHT: disputed variant of "all right" not yet widely accepted as correct

  Joanne was feeling <u>all right</u> until she saw her midterm grade.

- CONSCIOUS: to be alert
  CONSCIENCE: recognition of right and wrong

  The first thing the paramedic did was to assess whether the man was <u>conscious</u>.

  He had a guilty <u>conscience</u> after stealing utensils from the hospital cafeteria.

- COUNCIL: a formal group made up of individuals with a common interest

  COUNSEL: to advise or provide comfort

  The Hospital Advisory Council met regularly in order to evaluate institutional protocol.

  In her psychology class, the funeral services student learned how to provide effective counsel to grieving clients.

- i.e.: Latin for *id est* ("that is," or "in other words")

  e.g.: Latin for *exempli gratia* ("for example")

  The pharmacist needed a monthly massage (i.e., she needed to relax).

  Jung-Hee enjoyed many aspects of health care (e.g., patient contact, research, and teaching).

- ITS: of or belonging to it

  IT'S: a contraction of "it is"

  It's not a good sign that your dog keeps scratching its ears.

- LAY: to put down; to place somewhere

  LIE: to be in a horizontal position

  Lay the book on the table before you lie down for a nap.

- LOSE: to misplace; to not win (v.)

  LOOSE: not tight (adj./adv.)

  The clasp on my necklace is loose; I'm afraid I might lose it.

- PRESCRIBE: to direct or order

  PROSCRIBE: to prohibit or forbid

  The doctor told the patient he would prescribe medication if symptoms persisted beyond a week.

  The pharmacy had to proscribe certain medications because of known health risks.

- PRINCIPAL: main or most important (adj.); a person who has authority (n.)

  PRINCIPLE: a general or fundamental truth

  His principal concern was the cost of the project.

  The textbook covers the basic principles of genetics.

- REGARDLESS: without regard or despite of

  IRREGARDLESS: non-standard (do not use this word)

  Regardless of their experience levels, all paramedics must be astute on the job.

- RESIDENTS: people who live somewhere
  RESIDENCE: refers to place

  The nursing home <u>residents</u> looked forward to visits from their relatives.

  The nurse wanted to buy a <u>residence</u> closer to his workplace.

- SIGHT: to see
  SITE: location
  CITE: make reference to

  At first <u>sight</u>, I was not impressed by the development plans for the new building <u>site</u>.

  In nursing school, Jennifer learned how to properly <u>cite</u> her research sources.

- THAN: used with comparisons
  THEN: at that time; next

  I'm doing better in math <u>than</u> I am in chemistry.

  I'll study chemistry first, and <u>then</u> I'll review my math notes.

- THEIR: belonging to them
  THERE: indicates location
  THEY'RE: contraction of "they are"

  <u>They're</u> moving <u>their</u> offices to that building over <u>there</u>.

- VAIN: proud of one's personal appearance
  VEIN: a blood vessel
  VANE: a blade

  He was so <u>vain</u> that he refused to have a bandage placed on the ruptured blood <u>vein</u>.

  The windmill's <u>vane</u> slowly rotated.

- WAIT: to stay
  WEIGHT: refers to mass

  Sheneika's family told her they would <u>wait</u> for her outside the x-ray room.

  The patients in the eating disorders clinic have their <u>weight</u> monitored closely.

- WHO: refers to people
  WHICH: refers to things and is used to indicate secondary or non-essential information
  THAT: refers to people or things and is used to indicate essential information

  It does not matter <u>who</u> arrives at the hospital cafeteria first.

  Hospital gowns, <u>which</u> are worn frequently, need to be washed regularly.

  The family <u>that</u> requested an obituary yesterday phoned earlier.

Find the errors in the following sentences.

1. Franklin was thrilled when he was excepted into the paramedicine program.

2. Take two Aspirins and lay down for an hour.

3. I think I did alright on the exam.

4. What are the common side affects of that medication?

5. Lupus is sometimes misdiagnosed because it's symptoms are often mistaken for the symptoms of other diseases.

6. The nurse had difficulty locating Darlene's vain.

7. Irregardless of your fear, you need to go to the doctor for an annual check-up.

8. Due to common concerns on the job, the Paramedics Association organized a Safety on the Road Counsel.

9. You must learn how to site sources correctly, or you will be accused of plagiarism.

10. The first thing the paramedic did was to determine whether the patient was conscience.

A is for AUDIENCE-APPROPRIATE

Consider the needs of your audience. An audience of medical professionals will be familiar with specialized terminology, and will expect and need information that the general public will not.

Tips for Determining the Needs of Your Audience

Ask yourself the following questions:

1. Who are my readers? (Consider such things as age, gender, occupation, economic/educational background, and political or religious beliefs.)

2. Why will they be reading this document?

3. What do they need to know?

4. What do they already know? What do I need to tell them?

5. How specialized should my language be? How formal or informal? Do I need to define any terms?

6. Will they read every word or scan for key information? How can I help ensure that my message is received?

TRY IT YOURSELF

The following passage is taken from the report of an emergency room physician after performing a stump appendectomy on a 34-year-old woman. The audience is the patient's family doctor. Rewrite the passage for a non-specialized audience, for example, the patient's husband.

> *The patient was brought to the emergency room by ambulance at 0300 hours, August 11, 2007, for investigation of severe abdominal pains, nausea, and vomiting. Physical examination revealed a soft mass in the lower quadrant of the abdomen. Blood examination showed leukocytosis (white blood cell count 11,600/mm3) and an elevated C reactive protein (CRP) level (4.7 mg/dl). Computed tomography (CT) and ultrasonography of the abdomen showed an intraluminal mass. A preoperative diagnosis of stump appendicitis was made on the basis of the CT study. Stump appendicitis is a rare clinicopathologic entity characterized by inflammation of the appendiceal remnant after incomplete appendectomy.*

T is for THOROUGH

In the health professions, it is important that all communication be thorough and complete to ensure the best possible care. Many patient notes omit essential information—for example, instead of writing simply that a patient walked 30 feet, the health care worker should include the information that the patient needed a walker and was displaying shortness of breath. Many insurance claims do not get paid because information is missing from medical notes. Incomplete documentation could also result in a negligence lawsuit; there is a saying in the health professions: "If it wasn't documented, then, legally, it wasn't done."

Tips for Making Your Writing Thorough

1. Make a checklist of all the information that your reader needs to know.

2. Include all measurements and specifications. Be specific.

3. Include all relevant proper names—of people, places, medications, etc.

4. Proofread carefully, looking for missed steps or gaps in logic or information.

5. Ask yourself: If you were unfamiliar with the information being communicated, would you have any questions?

The following is an excerpt from a letter to an insurance company, asking for compensation. It is missing crucial information. Rewrite the paragraph, adding any missing details that you consider to be important.

The other week, while driving along Locust Street, I was hit by another car. My rear bumper was badly dented. The driver of the other vehicle was very apologetic and told me that she would take me to the hospital. I have severe whiplash and will have to stay home from work for a while.

The following two pieces of writing illustrate the difference between a personal narrative and an objective account that corresponds with the eight principles discussed above. The first piece (Box 2.1) is a short personal narrative in which a student recounts the events surrounding her sister's injury; the second piece (Box 2.2), recounts a fall in the form of a workplace INCIDENT REPORT that is clear, objective, concise, organized, accurate, correct, audience-appropriate, and thorough.

BOX 2.1	**Personal Narrative**

When my sister Gillian was about four years old, she smacked her head on the stairs to our basement and cut her eyebrow open. Gillian, my brother, and I were all in the basement watching TV when my mother called us up for lunch. We all bounded up the steps. My brother and I reached the top before my sister because she wasn't as fast as us, so we pushed her out of the way and went to the kitchen. She decided to go up the stairs on her hands and feet like a dog; one of her hands missed a step and she slipped off the stair and smashed her face onto the concrete stairs. She had hit the stair pretty hard, so she was dizzy and fell down the five or six steps she had already climbed. My mom heard her crying and ran to help her. When my mom saw that the stairs were covered in blood, she panicked. The gash in Gillian's head was so deep that we could see her skull. At the hospital, the doctor stitched her up and said that she was lucky because she could have fractured her skull. She had a lot of bruising on her face but was otherwise fine. She got some kind of anti-inflammatory pills to help with the pain and took a week off school.

TO:	Greg Kelley, Principal of Queen of Heaven Elementary School
FROM:	Kim Black, Witness
DATE:	September 21, 2007
SUBJECT:	Report of incident (20/09/2007) in which Gillian Orsini was injured.

Gillian Orsini sustained an injury above her right eye on September 20, 2007, in an accident that occurred at Queen of Heaven Elementary School at 1093 Gardner Avenue in Mississauga.

The accident occurred at approximately 12:30 p.m., when Ms. Orsini was walking up the flight of stairs in the northwest wing by the student cafeteria.

Halfway up the flight of steps, Ms. Orsini slipped and fell. The right side of her face hit the sixth concrete step. She then proceeded to fall down the five lower stairs, landing face down at the base of the staircase.

Immediately after Ms. Orsini fell, I, Kim Black, came to her aid. Ms. Orsini was bleeding from a three-inch wound above her right eyebrow. I gave Ms. Orsini some Kleenex from my purse; she proceeded to control the bleeding by applying pressure to the wound. I escorted her to my car and took her to Trillium Health Centre at 100 Queensway West.

We arrived in the Urgent Care Centre at 1:30 p.m. Ms. Orsini's wound was stitched and bandaged at approximately 2:15 pm. According to the attending physician, Dr. K. Smith, in addition to severe facial bruising on her right forehead, cheek, and chin, she has a one-half inch deep laceration above her right eyebrow.

Dr. Smith prescribed Tylenol 3 for seven days to help ease Ms. Orsini's pain and discomfort. He advised that the medication will make her drowsy. Therefore, for the duration that Ms. Orsini will be on the medication, she will not be able to attend school. Dr. Smith said she may return to classes after one week, or on approximately September 28, 2007.

Sincerely,

Kim Black

Kim Black

Exercise

1. Write a subjective, first-person account of an incident that you either experienced or witnessed. You should use the first person (*I*) and include your observations, thoughts, and feelings about the experience.

2. Exchange it with a partner, and read each other's accounts, looking for **clarity, objectivity, conciseness, organization, accuracy, correctness, audience-appropriateness,** and **thoroughness.** Highlight or underline the words and passages that need to be changed.

3. Then, return each other's papers and edit your own, transforming it into a **clear, objective, concise, organized, accurate, correct, audience-appropriate,** and **thorough** account of the incident.

I remember volunteering in a funeral home once where the owner got into a lot of trouble and embarrassment. One of the monuments the Home was responsible for had several writing errors on it. The deceased's surname was misspelled and the one-sentence tribute on the stone had a punctuation error in it; as well, the word "effected" was used instead of the word "affected." Now that I've graduated, I work in the industry and take great pains to carefully write down and verify all information about my clients. Dealing with loss and grief is hard enough. Silly writing errors on a tombstone add terrible insult to the already injured.

—Funeral Service Education graduate (Mount Royal University)

THE IMPORTANCE OF GRAMMAR

In addition to applying the properties of COCOACAT to your writing, you also need to use correct grammar. The following section gives a basic overview of common grammar errors in the areas of subject–verb agreement, pronoun usage, sentence errors, and modifier placement. Proper punctuation use as it applies to commas, semicolons, colons, and apostrophes is also reviewed. The grammar rules presented in the following section are the most commonly misunderstood or abused ones. English grammar can be quite complex and often contains exceptions. As such, your instructor may choose to elaborate on or present some of the more advanced and complex features of a rule.

SUBJECT AND VERB AGREEMENT

In a sentence, a subject must agree in number with its corresponding verb. In other words, a singular subject must be attached to a singular verb, and a plural subject must be attached to a plural verb. In the third person, singular verbs can often be distinguished from plural verbs because many of them end in *s*.

Ex.:

- *The <u>nurse eats</u> in the cafeteria.*

  (There is one nurse, so the singular form of the verb is used.)

- *The <u>nurses eat</u> in the cafeteria.*

  (There is more than one nurse, so the plural form of the verb is used.)

Preventing Subject–Verb Agreement Errors

In order to prevent common errors in subject–verb agreement, you need to pay special attention to the following circumstances: 1) subjects joined by *and*; 2) subjects joined by *or*; 3) indefinite pronouns; 4) countable or non-countable items; and 5) units of time, measurement, weight, and money.

1) Subjects joined by *and*

Two or more subjects joined by *and* take a plural verb.

Ex.:

- *The needles <u>and</u> bandages ~~falls~~ <u>fall</u> on the floor.*
- *Many of the nursing <u>and</u> paramedic students ~~was~~ <u>were</u> in the same writing class.*

  Write three sentences that demonstrate this rule.

1. _____
2. _____
3. _____

2) Subjects joined by *or*

Two singular subjects joined by *or* require a singular verb.

Ex.:

- *Either James <u>or</u> Jennifer ~~take~~ <u>takes</u> the night shift.*
- *A physiotherapist <u>or</u> chiropractor ~~keep~~ <u>keeps</u> the body functioning.*

  Write three sentences that demonstrate this rule.

1. _____
2. _____
3. _____

When the conjunction *or* joins a singular and plural subject, the subject closer to the verb determines the number of the verb.

Ex.:

- *The stethoscope <u>or gloves</u> ~~needs~~ <u>need</u> to be removed from the table.*
- *The gloves <u>or stethoscope</u> ~~need~~ <u>needs</u> to be removed from the table.*

  Write three sentences that demonstrate this rule.

1. _____

2. _____

3. _____

3) Indefinite pronouns

The words *each*, *either*, and *neither*, along with words that end in *one*, *thing*, and *body*, are called indefinite pronouns and require singular verbs.

Ex.:

- <u>*Everyone*</u> ~~are~~ <u>is</u> *learning a lot at the health convention.*
- <u>*Something*</u> ~~have~~ <u>has</u> *to change or the patients will be the ones to suffer.*
- <u>*Each*</u> *Health Sciences instructor* ~~deliver~~ <u>delivers</u> *material at his or her own pace.*

  Write three sentences that demonstrate this rule.

1. _____

2. _____

3. _____

The indefinite pronouns *both*, *few*, *many*, and *several* use plural verbs.

Ex.:

- <u>*Both*</u> *pharmacists* ~~takes~~ <u>take</u> *upgrading courses at the University of Toronto.*
- <u>*Few*</u> *students in funeral services* ~~does~~ <u>do</u> *not pass their program.*

  Write three sentences that demonstrate this rule.

1. _____

2. _____

3. _____

4) Countable or non-countable items

Some, *half*, *most*, and *all* take either singular or plural verbs depending on whether the word they refer to is countable or non-countable.

Ex.:
If they refer to a non-countable word, use a singular verb.

- *Some of the underline{milk} in the cafeteria ~~taste~~ tastes funny.*
- *All of the media underline{attention} ~~are~~ is annoying for the hospital.*

If they refer to a countable word use a plural verb.

- *Some of the underline{sandwiches} in the cafeteria ~~tastes~~ taste funny.*
- *All the underline{parking spots} around the hospital ~~is~~ are expensive.*

Write three sentences that demonstrate this rule.

1. _____

2. _____

3. _____

5) Time, weight, and money

Units of time, weight, measurement, or money usually take singular verbs.

Ex.:
- *underline{Three hours} ~~are~~ is a long time to wait for surgery.*
- *underline{Ten kilograms} of weight ~~take~~ takes a long time to lose.*
- *underline{Five dollars} ~~make~~ makes a difference when you are trying to save money.*

Write three sentences that demonstrate this rule.

1. _____

2. _____

3. _____

PRONOUNS

Pronouns are words that take the place of nouns. Their main function is to cut down repetition. See Box 2.3 for a list of common pronouns.

Preventing Pronoun Errors

In order to master pronoun usage, you need to pay particular attention to three key areas: **1) clarity, 2) number,** and **3) case.**

1) Clarity

Vague pronoun usage is a common error. It must ALWAYS be clear what a pronoun in a sentence refers to.

Ex.:

- *The nurse loved to go to Austrailia for her holidays; <u>they</u> were all so friendly.*

    Who does "they" refer to? The Australians? The animals? The tourists?

Fix:_____

- *I want to be a paramedic, but I am not good at <u>it.</u>*

    Not good at what? Driving? Thinking quickly? Dealing with injury?

Fix:_____

Clarify the pronoun reference(s) in the sentences below

1. Remove the gauze from the cabinet and replace it immediately.

    _____

2. The lecture hall was full of students and professors; they were especially attentive.

    _____

3. He was carrying juice, bread and cereal to the patient when he dropped it.

    _____

2) Number

A pronoun has to agree in number with the noun it refers to. As in subject–verb agreement, you need a singular pronoun if you are referring to a singular noun, and you need a plural pronoun if you are referring to a plural noun. As with subject–verb agreement, the *one*, *thing*, and *body* words, along with *each* and *either*, are considered singular. Box 2.3 reviews singular and plural pronoun forms.

Ex.:

- The _funeral director_ arranged for a grief counselor at ~~their~~ _his_ premises.
- The _patient and her mom_ left ~~her~~ _their_ coats in the waiting room.
- _Each_ brought ~~their~~ _his or her_ notebook to chemistry class.
- _Everyone_ in the class has ~~their~~ _his or her_ own lunch.

Write three sentences that demonstrate this rule.

1. _____

2. _____

3. _____

BOX 2.3 | **Pronoun Number and Case**

SINGULAR		
SUBJECT PRONOUNS	**OBJECT PRONOUNS**	**POSSESSIVE PRONOUNS**
I	me	mine
you	you	yours
he	him	his
she	her	hers
it	it	its
PLURAL		
we	us	ours
you	you	yours
they	them	theirs

3) Case

Pronouns can be used as a) subjects, b) objects, or c) possessives.

    a)   Subject: If the pronoun functions as the subject in a sentence, use a subject pronoun (_I, you, he, she, it, we, they_).

Ex.:

- *<u>She</u> is happy with the nurse.*
- *There were many times <u>he</u> felt frustrated by the health care system.*

Write three sentences that demonstrate this rule.

1. _____

2. _____

3. _____

b) Object: If the pronoun functions as the object of a sentence (it does not act as a subject), use an object pronoun (*me, you, him, her, it, us, them*).

Ex.:

- *After the staff meeting, Mary took <u>me</u> for coffee.*
- *We bought <u>him</u> a gift when he graduated from the physiotherapy program.*

Write three sentences that demonstrate this rule.

1. _____

2. _____

3. _____

c) Possessive: If the pronoun suggests ownership or possession, use a possessive pronoun.

Ex.:

- *The medication on the counter is <u>hers</u>.*
- *It is <u>mine</u>, but you may borrow it.*

Write three sentences that demonstrate this rule.

1. _____

2. _____

3. _____

Note that possessive pronouns NEVER contain apostrophes. See Box 2.4 for proper possessive pronoun forms, as well as nonsense forms that should be avoided.

BOX 2.4 — Possessive Pronouns

RIGHT	WRONG
yours	your's
hers	her's
its	it's (this form exists but is not a possessive pronoun)
mine	mine's
theirs	their's
ours	our's
NONSENSE PRONOUNS	
hisself, ourselfs, yourselfs, theirselfs, or themselves	

FAQs about Pronouns

Question: Is it "between you and me" or "between you and I"?

"Between you and me" is correct. *I* is a subject pronoun and cannot be used in cases where the pronoun does not act as a subject.

Ex.:

- *Between you and <u>me</u>, that instructor is disorganized.*

Question: What is the difference between who and whom?

Who is a subject pronoun and *whom* is an object pronoun. Use *who* if the word acts as a subject, and use *whom* if the word does not act as a subject or is acts as an object.

- *<u>Who</u> is looking after the patient?*
- *To <u>whom</u> should this fax be addressed?*

FRAGMENTS, RUN-ONS, AND COMMA SPLICES

Often, groups of words that are not complete sentences are mistaken as such. Sentence errors are generally divided into three categories: 1) **sentence fragments**, 2) **run-ons**, and 3) **comma splices**.

1) Sentence fragments

Every sentence must contain three components: a) a subject, b) a verb, and c) a complete thought.

  a) subject: the doer of the action or the thing associated with a state of being
  b) verb: an action or state of being
  c) complete thought: the connection between the subject and the verb should create a complete thought or whole idea

A sentence fragment is a group of words missing one or more of these three requirements.

Ex.:
  • *Always rushing. The paramedic needed to manage her time better.*
  • *Pharmacists have to carefully check prescriptions. Or a mistake occurs.*
  • *Listening skills are crucial for health care workers. Not an easy skill to master.*

Underline the fragment in each of the above passages.

2) The run-on sentence

This error occurs when two or more complete sentences are joined without proper (or any) punctuation.

Ex.:
  • *The nurse checked the patient's vital sign she became concerned.*
  • *The two paramedics were best friends they still argued at times though.*
  • *Sports injuries account for a lot of hospital visits every year the ER sees many cases.*

Underline the run-on error in each of the above sentences.

3) The comma splice

This occurs when two or more complete sentences are joined by a comma (commas are not strong enough to join sentences).

  • *The nurse checked the patient's vitals, she became concerned.*
  • *The two paramedics were best friends, they still argued at times though.*
  • *Sports injuries account for many hospital visits, each year the ER sees many cases.*

Underline the comma splice error in each of the above sentences.

Preventing Sentence Errors

1) The fragment

Always double check to make sure your sentences contain all three requirements of a complete sentence: subject, verb, complete thought. If any three of these components are missing, you need to revise accordingly.

2) The run-on and comma splice

Runs-ons and comma splices can be avoided and fixed using the same strategies. Note how the run-on and comma splice below are fixed using the five strategies that follow.

Ex.:
- run-on: *The patient asked the nurse to see her chart she was concerned.*
- comma splice: *The patient asked the nurse to see her chart, she was concerned.*

a) Make two simple sentences.

- *The patient asked the nurse to see her chart. She was concerned.*

Fix the sentences below using the "simple sentence" fix.

1. The nurse checked the patient's vitals she documented the results carefully.

_____

2. The two paramedics were best friends, they still argued at times though.

_____

3. The dressing needs to be changed everyday an infection might otherwise occur.

_____

b) Separate the complete sentences with a coordinating conjunction, also known as a FANBOYS (see Box 2.5). Whenever you use a FANBOYS to separate two complete sentences, you must place a comma before the FANBOYS in order to avoid a run-on error.

- *The patient asked the nurse to see her chart, for she was concerned.*

Fix the sentences below using the "FANBOYS" fix.

1. The nurse checked the patient's vitals she documented the results carefully.

_____

2. The two paramedics were best friends, they still argued at times though.

_____

3. The dressing needs to be changed every day an infection might otherwise occur.

_____

Coordinating Conjunctions (FANBOYS)

ACRONYM	COORDINATING CONJUNCTION
F	FOR
A	AND
N	NOR
B	BUT
O	OR
Y	YET
S	SO

c) Separate the complete sentences with an adverbial conjunction (also called a "conjunctive adverb"). See Box 2.6 for a list of common adverbial conjunctions.

- *The patient asked the nurse to see her chart; furthermore, she was concerned.*

Note how the adverbial conjunction "furthermore" is preceded by a semicolon and followed by a comma.

Fix the sentences below using the "adverbial conjunction" fix.

1. The nurse checked the patient's vitals she documented the results carefully.

_____

2. The two paramedics were best friends, they still argued at times though.

_____

3. The dressing needs to be changed everyday an infection might occur otherwise.

_____

BOX 2.6 — Common Adverbial Conjunctions (Conjunctive Adverbs)

accordingly	instead
additionally	likewise
also	meanwhile
besides	moreover
comparatively	namely
consequently	nevertheless
finally	next
further	nonetheless
furthermore	otherwise
elsewhere	rather
hence	similarly
however	subsequently
in addition	then
in comparison	thereafter
in contrast	therefore
indeed	thus

d) Separate the complete sentences with a semicolon.

- *The patient asked to see her chart; she was concerned.*

Fix the sentences below using the "semicolon" fix.

The nurse checked the patient's vitals she documented the results carefully.

_____

The two paramedics were best friends, they still argued at times though.

_____

The dressing needs to be changed everyday an infection might occur otherwise.

_____

e) Rewrite the sentence using a subordinating conjunction. See Box 2.7 for a list of common subordinating conjunctions.

- *Because the patient was concerned, she asked the nurse to see her own chart.*

Fix the sentences below using the "subordinating conjunction" fix.

1. The nurse checked the patient's vitals she documented the results carefully.

_____

2. The two paramedics were best friends, they still argued at times though.

_____

3. The dressing needs to be changed everyday an infection might occur otherwise.

_____

BOX 2.7	**Common Subordinating Conjunctions**

after	now that
although	once
as	since
as soon as	since
because	the first time
before	though
by the time	unless
even if	until
even though	when
every time	whenever
if	whereas
in case	whether or not
in the event that	while
just in case	while

MODIFIERS

Modifiers are groups of words used to limit, describe, or qualify other words. They can be single words, clauses, or phrases.

Ex.:

- *The nurse <u>warmly</u> greeted the patient.*
- *The lecture <u>that is taking place in E-135</u> is for funeral services students.*
- *The pills <u>on the counter</u> fell when the pharmacist turned around too quickly.*

What is being modified by the underlined words/phrases in the sentences above?

1. _____

2. _____

3. _____

Preventing Modifier Errors

Modifiers must be placed as close as possible to the item they are modifying in order to prevent error or misreading. Modifier errors generally fall into two categories: 1) **misplaced modifiers** and 2) **dangling modifiers**.

1) Misplaced modifiers

When a modifying phrase in a sentence is placed in such a way that it qualifies or modifies the wrong item, you have a misplaced modifier. To fix misplaced modifiers, move the problem phrase as close as possible to the item it qualifies in the sentence.

Ex.:

- *The patient put his valuables in the bag <u>that was suspicious</u>.*

(sounds like the bag was suspicious)

Fix:_____

- *The receptionist who sat behind the counter <u>with a soft voice</u> was difficult to hear.*

(sounds like the counter had a soft voice)

Fix:_____

- *She placed the picture on the table next to the hospital bed <u>of her dog</u>.*

(sounds like the dog had a hospital bed)

Fix:_____

2) Dangling modifier

Dangling modifiers occur when the subject of the modifying phrasing is unclear, missing, or misrepresented. These errors often occur (but not exclusively) when participial phrases (phrases with -*ing* words) are placed at the beginning of sentences. The subject following the modifying phrase must LOGICALLY be able to perform the action; otherwise, you have a dangling modifier.

- *Walking down the hall, the hospital robe got caught under his feet.*

  (sounds like the hospital robe was walking down the hall)

Fix:_____

- *While playing soccer with his friends, the ambulance sped by.*

  (sounds like the ambulance was playing soccer)

Fix:_____

Write three sentences that demonstrate this rule.

1. _____
2. _____
3. _____

- *After graduating from university, his high marks helped him secure work as a physiotherapist.*

  (sounds like his high marks graduated from university)

Fix:_____

COMMAS

Commas are one of the most commonly used punctuation marks, so it is important to use them properly. They serve a variety of functions in sentences, including indicating a pause, marking off non-essential information, or acting as the word "and" in lists.

Preventing Comma Errors

To use commas properly, pay particular attention to how they are used in the following circumstances: **1) coordinating conjunctions; 2) introductory material; 3) items in a series; 4) secondary information; 5) contrasts; 6) quotations; and 7) dates.**

1) Coordinating conjunctions (FANBOYS)

Commas precede coordinating conjunctions (FANBOYS; see Box 2.5, p. 41) when placed between complete sentences. If a FANBOYS does not separate a complete

sentence, a comma is not used. A comma is also not necessary if a FANBOYS separates two complete sentences that are very short, but it is better to include it.

Ex.:
- *Many nursing students went to the pub after lectures, but I did not go.*
- *Many nursing students went to the pub but I did not.*

Write a sentence using each of the FANBOYS that demonstrates this rule.

For _____

And _____

Nor _____

But _____

Or _____

Yet _____

So _____

2) Introductory elements

Commas follow introductory elements: a word or group of words that comes before a COMPLETE sentence.

Ex.:
- *First, the speaker talked about how best to serve the needs of patients.*
- *At the end of my shift, I just wanted to soak my feet and watch television.*
- *Driving the ambulance quickly, the paramedic learned to have good reflexes.*
- *Even though working with the sick was difficult, Ricardo loved interacting with patients.*

Write three sentences that demonstrate this rule.

1. _____

2. _____

3. _____

3) Items in a series

Commas separate items in a series (three or more items) that have equal rank or importance. The comma before the last item in a series is optional and referred to as the "Oxford comma."

Ex.:

- *The patient complained of pain, nausea, and diarrhea.*
- *The paramedic students had to take biology, chemistry and math.*

Write four sentences that demonstrate this.

with Oxford comma

_____

with Oxford comma

_____

without Oxford comma

_____

without Oxford comma

_____

4) Non-essential information

Commas set off unnecessary or parenthetical information (non-essential clauses). Common indicators of non-essential clauses include relative pronouns like *where*, *which*, *when*, and *who*. To determine whether information is non-essential in a sentence, ask yourself the following three questions. If you answer yes to one or more of these questions, it is likely that you are dealing with a non-essential clause.

- Will the sentence still make sense if the clause is removed?
- Does the clause interrupt the main idea of the sentence?
- Can the clause be moved elsewhere in the sentence without compromising meaning?

Ex.:

- *We will, nevertheless, go to the conference as planned.*
- *Diane, the nurse with black hair, always has a smile on her face.*
- *The young man, who was only 22, fractured his collar bone in a car accident.*
- *The north exit, which leads to the maternity ward, is closed.*

Write three sentences that demonstrate this rule.

1. _____

2. _____

3. _____

Do not enclose in commas any information that is essential to the meaning of the sentence (essential clause). *That* clauses, which often follow nouns or verbs, always signal an essential clause. In other words, while *which* is often preceded by a comma, the word *that* is not.

- *Students <u>that plagiarize</u> will be seriously disciplined.*
- *Documentation <u>that is sloppy</u> is unacceptable.*

Write three sentences that demonstrate this rule.

1. _____
2. _____
3. _____

5) Contrasting elements

A comma can be used to set off contrasting elements or an abrupt turn in a sentence. The words *not, instead, rather, though,* and *although* often indicate contrast or an abrupt switch.

Ex.:
- *The paramedic asked for coffee<u>, instead of tea.</u>*
- *Physiotherapy is a long term process<u>, not a quick fix.</u>*

Write three sentences that demonstrate this rule.

1. _____
2. _____
3. _____

6) Direct quotes

Commas set off direct quotes but not indirect quotes.

Ex.:
- *She said<u>,</u> "The pain gets worse each day."*
- *She told me that her pain gets worse each day.*

Write three sentences that demonstrate this rule.

1. _____
2. _____
3. _____

7) Dates

Use commas when writing dates. You do not need a comma when only the month and year are given, however.

- *The patient listed <u>March 10, 1975,</u> as her birth date.*
- *The patient was born <u>March 1975</u>.*

Write three sentences that demonstrate this rule.

1. _____

2. _____

3. _____

See Box 2.8 for common misuses of the comma.

| BOX 2.8 | Common Misuses of the Comma |

NEVER INSERT A COMMA	EXAMPLES OF MISUSE
... after a preposition	*Place the chart in, the tray when you are finished.*
... between a subject and its verb	*Denise, shifted the patient's shoulder as she had been taught.*
... between an adjective and its noun	*Samir looked forward to seeing the nice, pharmacist; she was so helpful.*
... between a verb and its object	*Austin does not like, midnight shifts.*
... after words like *such as* or *especially*	*I like many aspects of health care especially, lifting people's spirits.*

THE SEMICOLON

The semicolon is similar to the period in that it is predominantly used to separate complete sentences. Semicolons are used in two main situations: **1) separating complete sentences** and **2) lists with internal commas.**

1) Separating complete sentences

You can use a semicolon when separating two complete sentences THAT ARE CLOSELY RELATED. Adverbial conjunctions (Box 2.6, p. 42) are often used when separating two closely related sentences. When using this structure, make sure you the adverbial conjunction is followed by a comma.

Ex.:

- *Working with grieving individuals is difficult; clients who have lost children are especially challenging.*
- *Working with grieving individuals is difficult; particularly, it is challenging to work with clients who have lost children.*
- *Cheyenne gave the patient a handout of recommended exercises; she hoped her patient would have the discipline to do them.*
- *Cheyenne gave the patient a handout of recommended exercises; furthermore, she hoped her patient would have the discipline to do them.*

Write four sentences that demonstrate this rule.

1. Do not use an adverbial conjunction

_____

2. Do not use an adverbial conjunction

_____

3. Use an adverbial conjunction

_____

4. Use an adverbial conjunction

_____

2) Lists with internal commas

Use a semicolon to separate items in a series that contain several internal commas or that might otherwise be confusing.

Ex.:

- *The head nurse scheduled James, in Ward 2, for Monday; Cho, in Ward 4, for Tuesday; and Dorina, in Ward 3, for Wednesday.*
- *Health care professionals need strong communication skills, written and oral; the ability to respond quickly, responsibly and confidently; and a disposition suited for the job.*

Write three sentences that demonstrate this rule.

1. _____

2. _____

3. _____

THE COLON

A colon translates into *such as* or *namely*. Use a colon after a complete sentence to introduce a 1) **list**, 2) **explanation or elaboration**, or 3) **quotation**. A COLON MUST BE PRECEDED BY A COMPLETE SENTENCE; however, what follows the colon does not have to be a complete sentence.

1) Lists

Use a colon to introduce a list. Remember, what precedes the colon must be a complete sentence.

Ex.:

- *His mom had requested the following items as she recuperated from surgery: a book, slippers, mints.*
- *The pharmacist checked all aspects of the prescription carefully: the date, medication name and the recommended dosage.*

Write three sentences that demonstrate this rule.

1. _____
2. _____
3. _____

2) Explanation or elaboration

A colon can also be used to introduce an explanation or elaboration of what comes before it. Remember, what precedes the colon must be a complete sentence.

Ex.:

- *She was worried about her knee surgery: wondered long it would take to heal completely.*
- *His plantar fasciitis was acting up: especially in the mornings.*

Write three sentences that demonstrate this rule.

1. _____
2. _____
3. _____

3) Quotations

You can use a colon to introduce a quotation. Remember, what precedes the colon must be a complete sentence.

Ex.:

- *The paramedic documented the patient's exact words: "I feel like I'm dying."*
- *When charting, the nurse always remembered what her college writing instructor told her: "Be clear and concise!"*

Write three sentences that demonstrate this rule.

1. _____

2. _____

3. _____

THE APOSTROPHE

The apostrophe is a commonly misused punctuation mark and indicates **1) contraction** or **2) possession**.

1) Contraction

Contractions are two words that have been shortened into one word in order to achieve a natural, informal, or conversational style. Contractions are commonly used in informal writing but should be avoided in formal writing. In a contraction, the apostrophe takes the place of the letter or letters that are deleted.

Ex.:

- *I'm (I am) not entirely convinced that the patient is getting better.*
- *Money doesn't (does not) matter if your health is too poor to enjoy it.*

Write three sentences that demonstrate this rule.

1. _____

2. _____

3. _____

2) Possession

Apostrophes are also used to indicate possession or ownership. When considering an apostrophe, ask yourself two questions.

1. Is an act of possession taking place? Hint: Something is possessive if it works with an *of* phrase.

Ex.:
- *the <u>instructor's</u> house=the house of the instructor*
- *the <u>paramedic's</u> uniform=the uniform of the paramedic*

2. If an act of possession is taking place, is the noun that is doing the possessing singular or plural? The placement of the apostrophe depends on whether you are working with a singular or plural subject.

Singular subjects are made possessive by adding an *'s*, even if a singular subject already ends in *s*.

Ex.:
- *The <u>nurse's</u> shift conflicted with her <u>child's</u> daycare hours.*
- *The <u>pharmacist's</u> education prepared him well for his job.*
- <u>*James's*</u> *dream was to be a nurse practitioner.*

Write three sentences that demonstrate this rule.

1. _____
2. _____
3. _____

Plural subjects that end in *s* are made possessive by adding an apostrophe only.

Ex.:
- *The <u>physiotherapists'</u> convention was an annual event.*
- *Throughout the program, the <u>students'</u> confidence increased.*

Write three sentences that demonstrate this rule.

1. _____
2. _____
3. _____

Plural subjects that do not end in *s* are made by possessive by adding an *'s*.

Ex.:
- *The <u>children's</u> mother was very sick.*
- *The <u>geese's</u> path was blocked by the ambulance.*

Write three sentences that demonstrate this rule.

1. _____
2. _____
3. _____

3) Compound possessives

If two or more nouns jointly possess something, add the apostrophe to the last noun ONLY.

Ex.:

- *Renata and Sam's* house was closer to the hospital than their former apartment.
- The end of semester gathering for the pharmacy students is taking place at *Roy and Dean's* apartment.

Write three sentences that demonstrate this rule.

1. _____
2. _____
3. _____

If two or more nouns each possess a separate thing, each noun should have it own apostrophe.

Ex.:

- *Jennifer's and Maria's babies* were both born at the same time.
- *Michael's and Phillip's cars* were ticketed for being parked in the clinic lot overnight.

Write three sentences that demonstrate this rule.

1. _____
2. _____
3. _____

See Box 2.9 for common misuses of the apostrophe.

BOX 2.9	**Common Misuses of the Apostrophe**

NEVER USE APOSTROPHES	EXAMPLES OF MISUSE
... to make words plural	These three prescription's need to be filled.
	They usually occupied the three corner table's in the hospital cafeteria.
... with verbs	The nurse eat's as quickly as she can in order to make it back to work on time.
	He drive's the ambulance quickly, but cautiously.

PRACTICE: EDITING EXERCISES

Now that you have had a chance to review important aspects of grammar and the writing process, attempt the following editing exercises that require you to apply the grammar and writing knowledge that you have gained in this chapter. You may need to review the grammar points presented earlier in order to complete the exercises successfully.

Exercise 1

The following short piece based on the article "Paramedic Actor by Day, Paramedic by Night," by Karissa Donkin, about Toronto paramedic and actor Ryan Richardson, contains **ten errors,** as listed below. See if you can find them all.

- 1 sentence fragment
- 1 comma splice
- 1 run-on sentence
- 1 subject–verb agreement error
- 1 commonly confused word
- 1 misplaced modifier
- 1 missing comma
- 2 punctuation errors (other than commas)
- 1 missing apostrophe

Toronto paramedic Ryan Richardson has an interesting part-time job, he is an actor who has appeared in shows such as *Flashpoint*, *Cracked*, and *Warehouse 13*…playing a paramedic!

Richardson, who started recently a full-time job with Toronto EMS, never intended to be an actor. In 2009 three years after graduating from Humber College, he had started a job with Medic One, providing on-site medical services at film shoots in Toronto. He was on the set of Warehouse 13, and when he said he'd be willing to go on camera, he was picked for a scene; helping to transport a character on a stretcher.

Since then, irregardless of the fact that he has no formal drama training, he has appeared in a number of different episodes he has found that playing a paramedic on TV is not that different from being one in real life. He has to act as if the actors were real patients. So it would look accurate.

"Many paramedics say they gets frustrated watching when procedures are done incorrectly. If I'm able to help that and make the procedures on camera a little bit more accurate: then thats a good thing," Richardson said.

Source: Adapted from "Paramedic actor by day, paramedic by night," by Karissa Donkin, 2013, June 28, Toronto Star. Retrieved from http://www.thestar.com/entertainment/television/2013/06/28/paramedic_actor_by_ day_paramedic_by_night.html

Exercise 2

The following short piece, titled "I'm No Hero, Says Pharmacy Worker Who Found Diluted Chemo Drugs," is about Peterborough pharmacy assistant Craig Woudsma. It contains **ten errors,** as listed below. See if you can find them all.

- 1 sentence fragment
- 1 comma splice
- 1 run-on sentence
- 1 pronoun error
- 1 subject–verb agreement error

- 1 commonly confused word
- 1 missing comma
- two punctuation errors (other than commas)
- 1 missing apostrophe

In the spring of 2013, a pharmacy assistant at a Peterborough hospital looked very closely at a label on an IV bag and made the discovery that uncovered a major healthcare scandal. Pharmacy assistant Craig Woudsma, who works at the Peterborough Regional Health Centre, noticed that the bags from a new supplier needed to be refrigerated. While those from the former supplier did not. Upon comparing the labels he noticed that the ones from the new supplier, Marchese Hospital Solutions, had less information on it; and that the numbers didn't match up with his worksheet.

His questions began a process that revealed that, over the course of a year, more then 1,000 cancer patients in Ontario and New Brunswick received diluted chemotherapy drugs. This discovery has led to a commissioned Health Canada report it may lead to further monitoring and regulations of pharmaceutical companies.

He don't think of himself as a hero, he says that paying close attention to labels and following up on anything that seems unusual is: "just part of the process, its part of our job, and it just happens that this check that we made had a broader impact than we certainly would have anticipated."

Source: Adapted from "I'm no hero, says pharmacy worker who found diluted chemo drugs," 2013, May 7, CBC News. Retrieved from http://www.cbc.ca/news/health/story/2013/05/07/chemotherapy-peterborough.html

Exercise 3

The following exercise provides a brief introduction to Rahul Singh and his disaster response team, GlobalMedic. The exercise contains **ten errors**, as listed below. See if you can find them all.

- 2 comma errors (misplaced or missing)
- 2 subject-verb agreement errors
- 1 fragment
- 1 apostrophe error
- 1 word choice error
- 1 comma splice
- 1 modifier error
- 1 pronoun error

Rahul Singh's home is in Canada but he has been around the world in a capacity that most people will never experience.

Singh is the founder of GlobalMedic (David McAntony Gibson Foundation), based in Toronto, Ontario, a small disaster relief organization. Although a relatively small aid organization, GlobalMedic is often one of the first response teams to arrive on a disaster scene. To date, the organization has attended to over 60 relief mission's in 30 different countries, including recent efforts in Haiti and Nepal.

The foundation offers three branches of disaster relief. GlobalMedic responds with medical aid, water and training; GlobalFire conducts search and rescue missions; and GlobalWater focuses on water purification programs in developing countries.

Singh's team includes close to 500 professional volunteer emergency workers who, in keeping with the humanitarian aims of the organization, use personal vacation time to volunteer for disaster relief missions. The organization is always looking for volunteers whether to fundraise behind the seen or for more front line disaster work.

Although a skilled paramedic, Singh did not have much NGO experience when he launched GlobalMedic in 1998, nonetheless, he has managed to help raise millions for global disaster relief. Saved countless lives and endured the front line stresses of some of the world's most crippling devastations.

In listening to Singh speak, his medical background as a paramedic becomes almost secondary to the heart, spirit and authentic passion he shows towards humanitarian work. Such authentic dedication, make him a global inspiration and a well-deserved recipient of prestigious awards like the Order of Ontario in 2012. Other honours bestowed upon Singh includes the Humanitarian of the Year Award (2006), Canada's Top 40 Under 40 (2009), and in 2010, *Time* magazine voted him one of The World's Most Influential People.

Singh is a stellar example of compassion at work. Additionally, he vividly demonstrates how a health professional can use their skills to transgress borders and create lasting change.

Source: "If you're a physiotherapist, B.C. wants you," by Virginia Galt, 2013, May 31, The Globe and Mail. *Retrieved from http://www.theglobeandmail.com/report-on-business/careers/career-advice/if-youre-a-physiotherapist-bc-wants-you/article12291542*

Exercise 4

The following exercise, based on the article "Choose Your Words Wisely," by Michelle C. Danda, discusses the power of words in health care. It contains **fifteen errors,** as listed below. See if you can find them all.

- 5 punctuation errors (missing or misplaced)
- 3 word choice errors
- 2 subject–verb agreement errors
- 2 comma splices
- 1 pronoun error
- 1 fragment
- 1 modifier error

As a front line health care worker, Michelle Danda knows firsthand the power language has in nursing. Working as a nurse in an acute psychiatric setting. Danda remembers co-workers referring to clients in derogatory ways. Terms like "addict," "junkie," "user," and "drug abuser" was written in colleague's charts, she heard similar language when interacting verbally with co-workers.

Through these experiences, Danda came to recognize that a caregivers personal beliefs about addiction were often transferred through biased language in the workplace; in such a way that it effected both the quality of care patients received as well as the attitude of other staff members.

Even though she now has a different role in mental health nursing Danda continues to encounter nurses whose language is biased and unprofessional. She remains aware that she to can be influenced by such language: so she makes a conscience and concerted effort to regularly reflect upon her perceptions about mental health and addiction in order to not, unintentionally, compromise client respect.

Danda hopes to use her role to help transform the derogatory language she hears as a front line health care worker into communication that is unbiased and empowering. As marginalized individuals are often not able to fully advocate for themself, she sees herself as crucial to their advocacy. Using appropriate, empathetic and compassionate language when treating clients are a good place to start, Danda has the right idea.

Source: Adapted from "Choose your words wisely," by Michelle C. Danda, 2013, April, Canadian Nurse. *Retrieved from http://www.canadian-nurse.com/index.php?option=com_content&view=article&id=916%3 Achoose-your-words-wisely&catid=7%3Acommentary&Itemid=34&lang=enMICHELLE*

CHAPTER LINKS FOR FURTHER EXPLORATION

- **Grammar Book (http://www.grammarbook.com)**

This site includes explanations related to grammar, punctuation, and other writing rules. It also presents online quizzes to assess your understanding of the writing information presented.

- **Grammar Girl (http://www.quickanddirtytips.com/grammar-girl)**

Mignon Fogarty's site discusses all things related to grammar, from the simple to the obscure. She takes a fun, playful approach and makes grammar accessible to those who may otherwise struggle with it.

- **Humber Writing Centre (http://www.humber.ca/liberalarts/node/191)**

This Humber Writing Centre website contains numerous resources and handouts related to the academic writing process as well as comprehensive handouts on many grammar points. The site also provides links to other writing centres and useful grammar websites.

- **University College (http://www.uc.utoronto.ca/writing-centre)**

This University of Toronto site provides useful handouts on many of the grammar points presented in this chapter including punctuation, sentence errors, and modifiers. It also offers general advice on Writing for the Sciences.

3

WRITING IN AN ACADEMIC SETTING

At the end of this chapter, you should be able to

- recognize and produce various types of documents commonly assigned in health sciences programs
- write effective academic documents, including summaries, critical analyses, academic essays, and academic reports
- conduct academic research, including determining the credibility of sources
- prepare and format a formal academic essay or report

INTRODUCTION

As employers in the health professions are realizing the importance of writing well, more college and university programs are placing a greater emphasis on writing. Many students enter their programs unprepared for the types of academic documents they will have to produce and are unfamiliar with the skills of summarizing, analyzing, persuading, researching, incorporating sources into their writing, or documenting sources. In the following chapter, you will learn tips and strategies for approaching some of the typical writing assignments in health-related programs, including summaries, critical analyses, essays, and reports.

THE WRITING PROCESS

While there is no set way of approaching the task of writing an essay or report, it is important to have some system of organization, or you may feel overwhelmed by what is expected of you. Consider the following approach, in the suggested order, as you plan and organize your research essay or research report.

- Choose a topic from the choices offered to you.
- Research your topic. Stay focused on the issue at hand, or you will end up having to sort through too much information. Record the bibliographical data, such as authors, titles, and page numbers, of any sources you feel are relevant to your purpose. This information is vital when it comes time to do your in-text citations and References page.
- Once you have done some preliminary research, establish your thesis or purpose statement. Based on the knowledge you have, and the research and reading that you have undertaken, you should have a clearly defined argument or perspective.
- Sort through the information you have recorded from your research, and use any quotations, facts, opinions, or statistics that specifically support your thesis or purpose.
- Compose an outline. Keep in mind that you will most likely have to adapt this outline as you embark on the writing process.
- Write at least two rough drafts, remembering to integrate information you found during the research process, and correctly citing all "outside" ideas with in-text references. Then prepare your final copy, complete with a References page (see p. 94).

Overcoming Writer's Block

All writers—even novelists, journalists, and others who write for a living—frequently experience times that they stare at a blank computer screen or empty page, and no words seem to come. When you have a writing assignment due but are experiencing writer's block, what do you do to overcome it? What has worked in the past? What hasn't worked? Discuss with members of your group and come up with a list of at least five tips for overcoming writer's block.

THE SUMMARY

In your college or university health program, you may be asked to write a summary of an article, chapter, or book.

> *One of the most difficult things I had to do as a first-year nursing student was write an annotated bibliography for a research paper. I knew how to prepare a list of references in APA format, but I had no idea how to summarize an entire*

book or academic article in a short paragraph. It took me many tries to get the summaries short enough; I think I spent more time writing the summaries than I did writing the actual paper!

—Nursing student, Vancouver, BC

A summary is a short restatement of the main idea and supporting points of a piece of writing (see Box 3.1 below and Box 3.2, p. 64). The length of a summary depends on the length of the original text; a summary of a book may be a page or two long, while a summary of a short article may only be a paragraph in length. The summary should not exceed one-third of the length of the original document.

The goal of writing a summary is to communicate the central argument, purpose, structure, main ideas, and supporting points of the original in a condensed form.

Writing a summary …

- trains you to recognize the main points of an argument; and
- allows you to condense complex ideas into simple, clear points.

BOX 3.1 | **Sample Article**

Assisted Suicide: Quebec Has Found a Flexible Approach to Euthanasia Law

By Sarah Jones

In the latest attempt to legislate euthanasia, Quebec introduced Bill-52 on June 12. Canada has previously tried to address euthanasia at the federal level, but the issue is too heavy to get off the ground. The House of Commons decisively rejected Bill C-384 on April 21, 2010—59 votes in favour and 226 against (though almost every Bloc Quebecois member supported the Bill).

By framing euthanasia as a medical, not criminal, matter, Quebec brings the debate into provincial jurisdiction. This is a smart move, given that waiting for the federal government to pass a similar bill is an act of futility. Canada has proven itself to be entirely unable to regulate abortion, a similarly controversial act that intersects criminal and medical law (federal and provincial jurisdiction). Abortion, like euthanasia, is too divisive for the federal government. And so, Canada has inconsistent abortion policies because guidelines are set by individual hospitals. The lack of regulation also means lost opportunities for oversight and data collection.

Bill-52 sets the law for physicians and institutions across Quebec and demands high standards for care and oversight. End-of-life care in Canadian hospitals is changing with or without adapting regulations; Quebec's transparency and oversight should be strongly encouraged.

On the other hand, by foisting the debate into the provincial arena, Quebec may run into some difficulty. Some have argued that Quebec's bill violates criminal law and is unconstitutional. It is suggested that physicians providing terminal sedation and medical aid in dying will be convicted of murder. Certain acts of euthanasia are clearly illegal—hastening death without consent (think of Tracy Latimer) is illegal. Bill-52, however, sets out a full staircase of steps to ensure that patients have provided genuine, unforced, unpersuaded, well-informed and lasting consent. While others insist it is clearly legal, it is at least open for debate.

The Criminal Code defines murder as knowingly causing, directly or indirectly, the death of a human being. Hastening death is murder. Yet, by that definition hospitals across the country get away with murder daily. Physicians administer doses of morphine, knowing the morphine will shorten life. Physicians remove life-support. Physicians knowingly and directly cause death. Yet physicians end their shifts and drive away from hospitals without being arrested on the way home.

In 1992, the Supreme Court found that the removal of life-support (deliberately ending the life of a patient) was not murder because the underlying illness killed the patient, not the physician. The next year, Sue Rodriguez pled for help committing suicide. A slim majority of the Court found that administering pain relief was legal (even if it hastened death) but that the intention of the physician determined the issue. If the physician administered the dose with the intention of easing pain (incidentally, killing the patient), the act was legal; however, if the physician administered the same dose to kill the patient (incidentally, ending the patient's pain) then it was illegal. The exact same act could be legal or illegal depending on the intention of the physician, under the so-called "doctrine of double effect." Since Ms. Rodriguez was petitioning for a physician to end her life intentionally, she was denied relief (though the physician that ultimately assisted with her suicide was never charged, let alone convicted).

Bill-52 regulates the acts of physicians *intentionally* ending life. The Bill therefore pushes the law one crucial step past the Supreme Court's 1993 ruling. However, judges have been picking away at the Rodriguez decision for ten years now, and it is crumbling.

Most significantly, last year Justice Lynn Smith of the British Columbia Supreme Court (admittedly the decision is not binding in Quebec, and is being appealed) found that the "preponderance" of evidence from ethicists across the country showed that the intention of the physician does not alter the ethics of an action like administering a fatal dose of morphine. Justice Smith found that the ban on assisted suicide was unconstitutional and granted Gloria Taylor, a B.C. woman with ALS, the right to assisted suicide that Ms. Rodriguez was denied. If Justice Smith's decision is upheld on appeal then it will create a strong precedent to extend

continued

the law. The wild card, should this issue reach the Supreme Court, is that Chief Justice Beverley McLachlin was one of four dissenting judges in the Rodriguez decision; she may well be in the majority this time around.

Whether Bill-52 sustains legal challenges is only part of the debate. It remains to be seen whether it will receive political support, support from physicians, disability activists and Quebec in general. However, it should not be counted out simply because it pushes the boundaries of the law. The law is flexible, it can take it.

Sarah Jones, BSc, MBHL, JD, is a lawyer with a background in bioethics. She currently works in Hamilton.

Source: From "Assisted suicide: Quebec has found a flexible approach to euthanasia law," by Sarah Jones, 2013, June 27, The Globe and Mail. Retrieved from http://www.theglobeandmail.com/commentary/assisted-suicide-quebec-has-found-a-flexible-approach-to-euthanasia-law/article12853839. Reprinted with permission from the author.

BOX 3.2 | ## A Summary of "Assisted Suicide"

In the article "Assisted Suicide: Quebec Has Found a Flexible Approach to Euthanasia Law," which was published in the *Globe and Mail* on Thursday, June 27, 2013, the author Sarah Jones discusses the issue of euthanasia in light of Quebec's Bill 52, which was introduced on June 12, 2013.

Bill-52 brings the debate into provincial jurisdiction, which, the author argues, has both pros and cons. On the one hand, this takes the issue out of the hands of the federal government, which has already rejected a similar bill and is unlikely to pass one in the future. On the other hand, the author points out that Quebec doctors who assist patients in dying may face future convictions for murder, as some have argued that the bill violates criminal law.

Although the author concedes that, according to the Criminal Code, hastening death does constitute murder, she argues that physicians wittingly hasten death every day by removing life support or administering morphine. To illustrate the complexity of the issue, she cites cases in which the boundaries of the law have already been challenged, including a 1992 case in which the Supreme Court found that the removal of life support was not illegal, because the illness—not the doctor's actions—was determined to have caused the patient's death.

Jones concludes that, while it is impossible to predict whether Bill-52 will receive support from politicians, the medical community, or disability activists, it is important that the issue not be discounted simply because it challenges the existing interpretation of the law.

Some Special Types of Summaries

An **abstract** (see Box 3.3 below) is a short overview of the main points of a document. Its purpose is to provide sufficient information for the reader to determine whether the article or book will be useful to his or her research. It is usually between 75 and 120 words in length and appears at the beginning of a document. When you are asked to write a research paper, you may be required to provide an abstract. For more information on writing an abstract, see page 84.

An **annotated bibliography** (see Box 3.4 below) differs from a standard bibliography (list of references) in that it provides a brief description for each source listed. Its purpose is similar to that of an abstract.

BOX 3.3 **An Abstract of "Assisted Suicide"**

In the article "Assisted Suicide: Quebec Has Found a Flexible Approach to Euthanasia Law," the author Sarah Jones discusses the issue of euthanasia in light of Quebec's Bill-52, which was introduced on June 12, 2013. Although many argue that it violates criminal law, Bill-52 brings the debate into provincial jurisdiction, thereby taking the issue out of the hands of the federal government, which has already rejected a similar bill and is unlikely to pass one in the future. Citing cases in which the boundaries of the law have already been challenged, including Sue Rodriguez (1993) and Gloria Taylor (2012), Jones ultimately concludes that it is important that the issue not be discounted simply because it challenges the existing interpretation of the law.

BOX 3.4 **An Annotated Bibliography Entry for "Assisted Suicide"**

Jones, S. (2013, June 27). Assisted suicide: Quebec has found a flexible approach to euthanasia law. *The Globe and Mail*. Retrieved from http://www.theglobeandmail.com/commentary/assisted-suicide-quebec-has-found-a-flexible-approach-to-euthanasia-law/article12853839

In the article "Assisted Suicide: Quebec Has Found a Flexible Approach to Euthanasia Law," the author Sarah Jones looks at the legal implications of euthanasia in light of Quebec's introduction of Bill-52. Citing previous cases—including those of Sue Rodriguez (1993) and Gloria Taylor (2012)—that have pushed the boundaries of the law, she argues that, although Quebec's Bill-52 challenges the law on physician-assisted suicide, this alone should not be enough to discount it.

Tips for Writing a Summary

1. Read the document once, from beginning to end. Do not summarize as you read; digest the entire piece of writing before attempting to summarize it.

2. Read the document again, underlining or highlighting the main points, or noting the main points on a separate page.

3. Divide the document into sections; each section should have a main idea.

4. Write one sentence that captures the piece's main argument or thesis. This is your summary's thesis statement; it should include the author's name, the title of the article, the topic of the original article, and the author's position on that topic.

5. Going through the article, compose one sentence for each section or main point and write them on a separate piece of paper.

6. Write one sentence that summarizes what can be learned from reading the article. This is your conclusion.

7. Read through your summary, checking for clarity, readability, transitions, and grammatical correctness. Check that you are not using the same wording as the author of the original text.

Note: For information on the distinction between summarizing and plagiarizing, see pp. 106–108.

TRY IT YOURSELF

1. Read the article "Improve Aboriginal Health Through Oral History" (Box 3.5 below) and write a 100- to 200-word summary. Now, condense it even further into a 75–120 word abstract. Finally, write a 25–50 word annotated bibliography entry.

2. Choose a chapter or article in one of your textbooks and write a 100- to 200-word summary.

BOX 3.5 | Sample Article

Improve Aboriginal Health Through Oral History

By Nicholas Keung

In 1965, a teenaged Rene Meshake was plucked away from his Aroland reserve in Northern Ontario and placed in a residential school.

For years, the Ojibway man suppressed his childhood memories of love, care, and indulgence because of the abuse and abandonment he experienced at the McIntosh and Fort Frances Indian schools.

"I remember the first rabbit I snared and skinned. Everybody just feasted on it. I was raised by the whole community," Meshake, now 62, recalls of his early years.

"But after the residential school, I was angry and depressed. I tried to block out all my memories by drinking," he said, pausing a moment. "I was afraid to trust again." Meshake later spent years being homeless in Toronto and often contemplated suicide.

Kim Anderson, a research associate with St. Michael's Hospital's Centre for Research on Inner City Health, said the residential school era not only disrupted the community's ability to build healthy relationships; it also robbed a generation of the opportunity to learn traditional parenting skills to raise their own healthy families, and ultimately contributed to the social ills faced by the community today.

"The residential school is the biggest and ugliest elephant in the middle of the room in terms of the disruptions," said the oral historian.

"Parenting skills were not passed on because there was no role modeling in these schools. We learn parenting by being parented. To top it all off, there was sexual and physical abuse. It added another dimension."

That is why Anderson has teamed up with colleague and family physician Dr. Janet Smylie—both are Métis—to establish the Indigenous Knowledge Network for Infant, Child and Family Health to uncover the lost traditions and develop culturally relevant health promotion strategies through aboriginal oral history.

"So far, European knowledge hasn't been making a big difference for aboriginal people. If you look at Northwestern Ontario, 30-plus of the communities over the last 15 years have seen a 20-fold expansion over access to western biomedicines—but their health outcomes are actually getting worse," said Smylie.

"Nobody is going to get better from a knowledge system that is very different from their own unless there is some kind of bridging. You have to work with people in a language and conceptual framework that fits for them," said Smylie. "Like any style of advertising and negotiation, you have to meet people where they are."

The five-year project involves 10 community partners in Ontario and Saskatchewan, where frontline health workers collect information from elders about lost skills and rituals in traditional parenting, pregnancy, labour and birth, and prenatal and postnatal care. They will then incorporate the knowledge in community health programming and practices.

Meshake was brought up by his grandparents and uncles, who taught him how to fish, hunt and live. All was good up until he was removed from the "res" (reserve).

He recalled his grandmothers would only wave a willow stick in front of his nose if he misbehaved, or use the threat of "Missabi" or Big Foot if he told a lie to teach him a lesson in honesty—a contrast to the stick beatings and strict discipline at the residential school.

When he left the residential school, Meshake never had a steady job or stable relationship and was rarely sober until he had an awakening in 1991.

"A friend of mine died. I went and buried him. I put the sand on his coffin and said to him, I'm burying my past with you," said Meshake, who has a graphic design diploma from Sheridan College and is now a published author and graphic artist.

continued

WRITING IN AN ACADEMIC SETTING

"The residential school has disrupted the whole patterns of the rite of passage. This has to do with healing, sealing things," he said. "And I've told myself I would never pass on my negative experience to my (now 15-year-old) son."

Pauline Shirt, a Cree great-grandmother in Toronto, is more fortunate growing up at the Saddle Lake Reserve in Alberta. She too attended a residential school but remained close to her parents and nine siblings.

"I was raised on my father's farm to take care of Mother Earth and the animals. I learned about all the teachings of the spiritual world," said Shirt, 66, who helps raise her three great-grandchildren in Toronto.

"We believe in the seven stages of life where we each have our roles to play in the community. But unfortunately, a lot of people became disconnected and were robbed of those teachings."

As an elder, Shirt teaches traditional knowledge to others in the community. She also founded the First Nations School of Toronto in 1977, which was then called Wandering Spirit Survival School.

"We have to start with our youth," said Shirt. "We will need to help each other to help ourselves."

The project is funded by the Canadian Institutes of Health Research and Ontario Federation of Indian Friendship Centres.

Source: From "Improve aboriginal health through oral history," by Nicholas Keung, 2010, May 2, Toronto Star. Retrieved from http://www.thestar.com/life/health_wellness/2010/05/02/improve_aboriginal_health_through_oral_history.html. Reprinted with permission—Torstar Syndication Services.

THE CRITICAL ANALYSIS

A critical analysis (see Box 3.6 and Box 3.7) is, like a summary, a condensed version of a longer piece of writing. However, unlike a summary, an analysis includes your evaluation of what you have read. The goals in writing an analysis are (1) to give an objective explanation of a written text, and (2) to give your carefully considered opinion on the author's views and on how successfully he or she has presented those views.

Writing a critical analysis ...

- trains you to read closely, and to understand what you read, rather than merely "skimming" the surface of a text;
- allows you to recognize the way a piece of writing is structured and to trace the development of the author's reasoning; and
- enables you to evaluate the strengths and weaknesses of an argument.

BOX 3.6

Sample Article

Brain Rewiring: Using Magnetic Fields to Treat Depression Is Gaining Favour

By Alexandra Shimo

Lying back in a spacious, leather armchair, Barbara Kwasniewski seems relaxed, especially given the nature of the medical treatment she's just received. The 53-year-old has undergone repetitive transcranial magnetic stimulation (rTMS), which essentially rearranges the pathways of the brain by using magnets.

The therapy was approved by Health Canada in 1997 and by the U.S. Food and Drug Administration in 2008. It's used to treat everything from strokes to depression, anorexia, migraines, obsessive-compulsive disorder, chronic pain and Parkinson's. It's one of a handful of therapies gaining popularity that use electricity to help rewire the brain. Deep brain stimulation is another, where wires are surgically implanted into a patient's grey matter to excite the neurons with electronic pulses. Electro-shock therapy has also made a comeback.

Of these electrical brain therapies, rTMS is the least invasive. Research is under way to determine its full potential: doctors aren't sure whether it's better to target one or both sides of the brain. They now stimulate just one side—the region depends on the disease—but this may change with further research. Nor have they determined how intense to make the magnetic field. If it's too strong, there is risk of causing a seizure. But if it's too weak, the treatment won't work. For these reasons, the therapy is regarded as experimental, says Dr. Gary Hasey, who started the first therapeutic transcranial magnetic stimulation lab in Canada in 1997.

What's groundbreaking about the treatment is that it can help people for whom all other options have failed. Studies show that about 40 per cent of these people improve, says Dr. Jeff Daskalakis, a psychiatrist who runs the brain treatment and research program at the University of Toronto. Kwasniewski fell into a deep depression 13 years ago, after giving birth to her daughter. She slept 18 or 20 hours per day. She tried every "antidepressant under the sun." Suicide was never far from her mind, and she would probably have gone through with it, she says, but for her daughter.

For the past three years, Kwasniewski has come to the Toronto-based Centre for Addiction and Mental Health (CAMH) for 20-minute sessions of rTMS. Twice a week, she sits in the big armchair. Next to the chair is a box with dials and knobs. Connected to the box is a black wire coil shaped like a figure eight. A nurse holds the coil to the top of Kwasniewski's head, just above the dorsolateral prefrontal cortex—an area of the brain responsible for planning and organization. When a current goes through the wire, it sets up a magnetic field, which is strongest at the point where the wires cross. The magnetic field excites the neurons underneath

continued

the coil, activating the pathways of her brain that inhibit negative thinking. The wire makes a clicking noise that sounds and feels, she says, like a woodpecker tapping at her skull. The known side effects of the treatment are seizures, headaches, and involuntary clenching of facial muscles, but so far, she's only suffered slight head pain after an early treatment.

In the public system, rTMS is available in Toronto, Hamilton, Vancouver, and Red Deer, but growing demand means the queues can be long; for example, at Toronto's CAMH, the wait is one year. The MindCare Centres offer the country's only private rTMS program, with clinics in Vancouver, Toronto, and Ottawa. A Montreal clinic opened just last week, and there's one more slated for Toronto. The cost is $5,000 to $7,500 for a course of treatment that lasts two to three weeks. The fees can be covered under insurance, although it's decided on a case-by-case basis. MindCare uses particularly strong magnets, setting the frequency above what has been tried in the research studies, and they report a higher success rate, with about 60 per cent of patients improving.

Every four months Bill Neill, 53, who lives in Oakbank, a suburb of Winnipeg, flies to Vancouver for a week of rTMS treatment at a MindCare Centre, which costs about $8,400 per year, including flights and hotels. Neill's doctors suggested he try rTMS because none of the anti-depressants eliminated his seasonal depression that was so serious that he used to take a leave from his job with Manitoba Hydro for a few months every year, and spend his days curled up in a ball, crying. He will probably need magnet therapy for the rest of his life, he says. "The cost is a stretch," says the father of three. "But it means I no longer live my life on a roller coaster." For Kwasniewski, the therapy has boosted her confidence and given her a renewed sense of purpose: her weight has fallen by 100 lb., and she has started to socialize again. Although there aren't any studies on how the therapy will affect her long-term health, she doesn't care. "If my brain turns to jelly in 20 years," she says partly in jest, "at least I will have had all those good years."

Source: From "Brain rewiring: Using magnetic fields to treat depression is gaining favour," by Alexandra Shimo, 2009, February 16, Maclean's, *p. 49. Reprinted with permission from* Maclean's *magazine.*

BOX 3.7   **A Critical Analysis of "Brain Rewiring"**

The article "Brain Rewiring," which appeared on *Macleans.ca* on February 9, 2009, was written to inform the general public about a controversial new treatment for depression. Author Alexandra Shimo explains the use of repetitive transcranial magnetic stimulation (rTMS) to treat depression and other conditions. While Shimo provides moving testimonials from two patients currently undergoing rTMS treatment for severe depression, and consults two doctors who perform the treatment, this article does not adequately explore the science behind the therapy, the controversies surrounding the therapy, or the possible short- and long-term effects of the therapy.

As Shimo explains, repetitive transcranial magnetic stimulation, also known as rTMS, works by altering the brain's pathways through magnets. The treatment has been approved in both Canada and the U.S. and can be used to treat a variety of conditions, including strokes, depression, obsessive compulsive disorder, chronic pain, and Parkinson's disease. While there are other electrical therapies available, rTMS is far less invasive than deep brain stimulation or electroconvulsive therapy. RTMS works by triggering the brain's neurons through the use of a magnetic field. This field, consequently, activates the part of the brain responsible for negative thinking.

While studies of the therapy's success so far indicate room for optimism, there are still some unanswered questions. Doctors are still unsure, for example, whether to apply the magnets on one or both sides of the brain, and they struggle with exactly how intense the magnetic field should be in order to be effective. In addition, the potential side effects of rTMS are seizures, headaches, and clenching of facial muscles. While the treatment is currently available in several Canadian cities, the waiting lists are long and the costs can be as high as $7,500. Still, for those who have undergone other treatment options for depression with little or no improvement, the author clearly feels that rTMS is a valid option.

In this article, Shimo focuses on the benefits of rTMS for treating depression; her evidence, however, is largely anecdotal, based on the experiences of two patients currently being treated with rTMS. Shimo's descriptions of how the treatment works are directed toward the non-specialist; the machine is described as "a box with dials and knobs," and the movement of the wire sounds and feels "like a woodpecker tapping at [the patient's] skull." Shimo mentions that there are questions regarding the intensity of the magnetic field, the best areas of the brain to target, and the short- and long-term side effects, but these are not pursued in her article. This article provides an overview of rTMS for a general readership and would be of very little use to health practitioners, other than as an introduction to the concept of rTMS.

Tips for Writing a Critical Analysis

1. Read the text.

2. Read it again, noting the following:

- the author's purpose in writing (to inform, to persuade, to compare, etc.);
- the intended audience; and
- the topic and the author's position on the topic.

3. Jot down the secondary arguments that support the main argument, along with the evidence used to support the arguments.

4. Ask yourself the following questions:
   - Is the main argument of the piece clearly stated?
   - Is the organization of the piece logical?
   - Are the points well-supported?
   - Has the author achieved his or her purpose?

5. Write down the weaknesses of the author's argument. What points do you agree with? What points do you disagree with? Give reasons for both.

Structure of a Critical Analysis

Introduction

Your introduction should include the author's name, the title of the article or book, and the year in which it was published. It should also include the author's purpose, audience, and main argument. Last, it should also contain your thesis, which consists of your opinion about what you have read.

Summary

The next paragraph summarizes the main points that the author uses to support his or her argument. Provide an objective overview of the argument and supporting points. Do not give your opinion at this point.

Analysis

Now, evaluate the piece of writing. Is it convincing? Is there enough support? Is the support strong enough? How effective is it? Back up your opinions with evidence from the text itself.

Conclusion

End by briefly stating your overall evaluation of the piece. Is it effective, and why or why not? Has the author achieved his or her purpose? Is this article useful to the audience for which it is intended?

TRY IT YOURSELF

1. Read the article "Improve Aboriginal Health through Oral History" (pp. 66–68), and write a 200- to 400-word critical analysis.

2. Choose a chapter or article in one of your textbooks, and write a 200- to 400-word critical analysis.

ESSAYS AND REPORTS

Robert Kneschke / Shutterstock

On your way to achieving the goal of being a skilled health professional, you first have to get through school. No matter what health science program you are enrolled in, it is highly unlikely that you will get through your program without having to write **essays** or **reports**.

What Is the Difference Between an Essay and a Report?

This is a very good question and one that is often debated among those who teach composition courses. While the answer is open to interpretation, some differences are generally agreed upon (see Table 3.1).

Generally speaking, reports deal with facts and are experiment-oriented while essays are opinion-oriented. This means that courses that focus on critical thinking, like literature and philosophy, often expect essays, while fact-based disciplines, like the sciences, encourage the writing of reports. Additionally, reports use **headings** to separate sections more often than essays do; essays tend to emphasize textual flow over section breaks. Table 3.1 contrasts common section requirements of essays and reports.

A common type of report found in the health sciences is a classification report. A classification report might ask you to classify fast food items in terms of fat content. In a report on this topic, your goal is to present facts in a structured and organized way, and then interpret these facts analytically and meaningfully.

TABLE 3.1 Contrasting the Essay and the Academic Report

	THE ESSAY	THE FORMAL ACADEMIC REPORT
PRESENTATION OF GOAL	Thesis statement	Purpose statement
		Objective
PARTS	Title page	Title page
	Introduction	Abstract
	Body	Table of Contents
	Conclusion	List of Figures
	References (if research essay)	List of Tables
		Introduction
		Literature Review
		Methods and Materials
		Results
		Discussion
		References
		Tables
		Figure Captions
		Figures
		Appendices
		Note: The exact sections required will be determined by the professor; APA format does not require a Table of Contents, List of Tables, or List of Figures.
SECTION BREAKS	Topic sentences	Headings
MISCELLANEOUS	Emphasized in the humanities	Emphasized in the sciences

Sometimes, however, your professors will require that you write an essay instead of a report. A persuasive essay, for example, is a type of academic essay commonly assigned in university and college courses (see Box 3.8 on p. 76). A student might, for example, be asked to argue his or her perspective on a debatable topic, such as the mandatory listing of nutritional information on all fast food menus.

Unlike the classification report mentioned earlier, where your goal is to provide factual information, here your purpose is to take a stance on whether nutritional information should or should not be listed on fast food menus. If your essay requires research, you would also have to integrate credible sources that support your particular stance on the subject.

APA Formatting

Essays and reports in the sciences are prepared according to the guidelines provided by the American Psychological Association (APA). Following all of these rules can be frustrating, but there are important reasons for doing so: formatting guidelines provide consistency and uniformity across a variety of disciplines, give your writing credibility among your professional peers, and remove the distraction of choosing how best to format the various parts of your document. The following are the main APA guidelines for formatting essays:

- Type your essay on 8½-inch by 11-inch white paper and use one side of the paper only.
- Double-space throughout your assignment.
- Leave 1-inch margins at the top, bottom, and sides of each page.
- Do not justify the right margin; leave it ragged.
- Use italics, not underlining, throughout.
- Type your essay in a common 12-point typeface like Times New Roman.
- Staple your essay or report in the top left corner. Do not use a binder or folder unless your instructor asks for one.
- Use Arabic, not Roman, numerals when numbering pages.
- Formal essays and reports must have a **title page**. The title page for a course paper includes the full report title, along with the author's name, course, professor, and date of submission (see the sample report on page 90). For a paper being submitted for publication, include only title, author, and institution. Make sure your essay or report title clearly describes the contents of your report. Do not put visuals on your title page.
- Use standard capitalization for your title: capitalize all words in titles except conjunctions, articles, and prepositions under 4 letters; capitalize first and last word of title and subtitle regardless of length.
- The title page also identifies the running head, at the top of the page, flush left, preceded by the words "Running head:"; a page number appears on the same line, flush right. The title page is page 1 of your paper.
- All pages of your report, with the exception of the title page, must include a **running head**, which consists of either the full or a shortened version of the essay or report title (use a shortened version if the title is longer than 50 characters), and a page number. The running head should be placed at the top of the page flush left, while page numbers are placed flush right.

In Chapter 4, we will address the APA conventions for documenting sources.

BOX 3.8 **Sample Persuasive Essay**

Demanding Transparency from the Fast Food Industry

Current food trends in Canada clearly point to a country where health and well-being matter. Judging from the growing organic food industry to packed exercise clubs, outdoor boot camps, and the numerous diet books sold in bookstores, looking good and feeling healthy seem to be a priority for many Canadians. To further this trend, there has been recent discussion in Canada concerning the implementation of laws that would require fast food restaurants to post nutritional information about the foods they sell. Canada should, indeed, enact nation-wide laws that require fast food restaurants to post nutritional information about their food products for three very good reasons: convenience, education, and health.

First, having access to nutritional information at the point of purchase is a convenient and effective way of providing consumers with important health information. In a 24/7 society, where banking and grocery shopping can be done at virtually any time, it seems that Canadians demand convenience, especially in urban areas where time is of the essence. The busy professional often finds him- or herself in a situation of having to "pick up" a snack or a meal, and the convenience of fast food restaurants, coupled with their affordability, makes fast food a practical option for many. While consumers might be able to access nutritional information about their favourite fast foods online, when craving a McDonald's Big Mac or a Dairy Queen Blizzard, they are unlikely to first "log in" in order to determine the fat content or caloric information of their favourite treat. The immediacy of nutritional information that is visible and accessible at the point of purchase may very well be the factor that motivates a consumer to make a healthier food choice.

Second, in a democratic society it is only right that citizens be educated on the foods that they ingest. While ignorance can be bliss, when it starts to affect health, knowledge is preferable. Canadians demand transparency in many aspects of their lives, including what politicians spend taxpayer dollars on and what kids are being taught in school, so it is only right that we expect restaurants to be transparent about the content of the foods they serve. If nutritional information reveals that a typical serving of soda contains 40 grams of sugar, would you still choose to ingest it? The fact is that while a good number of Canadians want to eat healthier, words like "monounsaturated" and "unsaturated" and the percentages and calculations that often appear on nutritional information tables seem to be a secret code that only a select few can interpret. Educating consumers on how to interpret nutrition labels, as well as informing consumers, in an accessible way, about the nutritional content of popular fast food products like burgers, fries, and milkshakes, might inspire healthier food choices. Some critics bring up the notion of free will and suggest that restaurants should not be forced to post such information. Despite the democratic principles that flourish in Canada, businesses are required to abide by laws all the time (sanitation and zoning laws, for example), so the argument against coercion is not a realistic one. The free will of the consumer would certainly not be affected by mandatory posting of nutritional information as it is the consumer who ultimately chooses, despite the posting of the information, whether to consume a product or not. In fact, the consumer is the one who makes the choice as to whether he or she even wishes to read the nutritional information in the first place.

Third, obesity appears to be a growing problem in North America and making it mandatory for fast food restaurants to post nutritional information may help in efforts to reduce obesity and other health complications associated with it. Obesity has been linked to poor self-esteem and bullying (particularly in youngsters), as well as to serious health complications like heart disease and hypertension. Consumers concerned about obesity or health risks associated with the regular consumption of fast foods may, indeed, select healthier items if provided with information on a particular food's nutritional value, or lack thereof. By accessing such information, consumers are able to make more informed choices. A comprehensive listing of a food's ingredients can also save individuals with food sensitivities great distress or possibly even death. Critics may argue that it has not been proven that the posting of such information would decrease obesity rates. However, it also has not been proven that such information would not curb obesity rates. As such, if the transparency of fast food nutritional content has the potential to make Canadians healthier, it seems reasonable to at least give it a try.

In conclusion, some states in the U.S. have already started to experiment with the mandatory posting of nutritional information at fast food restaurants and Canada should as well. Convenient access to health information as well as transparency in what we ingest has the potential to lead to healthier food choices, and healthier food choices may help in efforts to curb obesity and those ailments associated with it. While a law proposing the mandatory listing of nutritional information at fast food establishments is not an all-encompassing and easy fix to problems concerning health and well-being, and would require significant planning, administration, and confrontations with "nay-sayers," the government should still take the time and effort to implement such measures based on the potential benefits that may arise. Given all the potential advantages of posting nutritional information, it is difficult to understand why nationwide laws supporting it have not already been implemented.

A third opening transition is used here.

The topic sentence introduces the main point of the third body paragraph: health.

The author, again, answers her critics here, providing further strength and validity to her argument in the process.

The transition "In conclusion" signals that the essay is about to come to a close.

The summary statement restates the author's thesis and appears at the beginning of the concluding paragraph.

The author closes with a thought-provoking statement.

WRITING IN AN ACADEMIC SETTING

THE ACADEMIC ESSAY: INTRODUCTION, BODY, AND CONCLUSION

The Introduction

The first paragraph in an essay is called the **introductory paragraph.** This paragraph introduces your topic and your viewpoint on that topic. Introductory paragraphs should move from the general to the specific: they begin by providing some general background on the topic, often through the form of definitions and other information that helps establish context. The essay introduction is the first thing your reader sees, so make sure that it effectively and accurately represents the contents of your essay. The most important part of the essay introduction, however, is the **thesis statement.**

DON'T

- Don't include specific examples or details in your introduction.
- Don't stray from the essay topic.

The Thesis Statement

The thesis statement expresses an argument about the topic that you are writing about. In undergraduate courses, professors usually encourage students to place the thesis statement at the end of the introductory paragraph. This means that the thesis statement is the most specific part of your introduction, recalling from our earlier discussion that the introduction flows from general to specific. While many students fear the thesis statement, writing one does not have to be intimidating or scary if you remember this simple, no-fail formula:

Essay topic + argument = thesis

Suppose, for example, that your professor wants you to write an essay based on the following essay topic:

Discuss the special predicaments male nurses face in the hospital setting.

The first step in creating a thesis based on this topic is to plug the right variables into the no-fail formula:

Topic = special predicaments of male nurses

Your argument = male nurses are stereotyped, they are discriminated against, and they lack support in the workplace

Then, combine the two parts together:

Male nurses in hospitals have to battle the following challenges: stereotypes, discrimination, and lack of psychological support.

You have just created a thesis statement.

If you look carefully at the above statement, you will notice that you not only created a thesis in response to the topic, but you did another very important thing in the process: you set up the organization of your paper. Your thesis statement shows that your essay's first section will deal with how male nurses are stereotyped, your second section will deal with how male nurses are discriminated against, and your third section will deal with how male nurses lack support to deal with their specific challenges. (In a short essay like this one, each section is a paragraph long.)

Strong thesis statements thus do at least two things: they express your argument clearly and concisely, and set up the organization of the piece of writing that follows.

Now that you understand what makes a strong thesis statement, it is equally important to avoid creating a weak one by paying close attention to the "Don't" list below.

DON'T

- Don't write an announcement

  In this essay, I will …
  The subject of this essay is …

- Don't write a thesis that is too broad for the length restrictions of your assignment

  All the paramedic programs at colleges around the world have high standards.

- Don't state a fact

  Canada's health care system is publicly funded.

- Don't argue points that are not unique and distinct

  Weak: *Regular cardio exercise benefits an individual's physical health, bone health, and emotional health.*

  In the statement above, the thesis points are not unique and distinct as bone health is part of overall physical heath. So, you need to rewrite your statement, making sure your thesis items are unique and distinct.

  Strong: *Regular cardio exercise benefits an individual's physical and emotional health.*

TRY IT YOURSELF

1. Indicate whether the following statements are good thesis statements for a 1000-word essay. Be prepared to defend your choice.

   a) There are problems with Canada's health care system.
   b) I will write about how H1N1 flu is spread.

c) Common triggers for anorexia nervosa include low self-esteem, media influence, and dysfunctional relationships.
d) Male nurses encounter more workplace challenges than female nurses.
e) To be a successful paramedic, one must be flexible, adaptable, and able to handle change.

The Body

All paragraphs within your essay with the exception of the opening and closing paragraphs constitute the essay **body**. The body of an essay is where you showcase the evidence and examples that support your thesis. The length of your essay's body depends upon the specific requirements of your assignment, but undergraduate programs are fond of the five paragraph model for shorter essays, which means that there are three body paragraphs framed by both an introduction and a conclusion. Each body paragraph must have a **topic sentence**. A topic sentence is a statement that appears at the beginning of each new paragraph and explains the contents of that particular paragraph.

Organization of the body

As you attempt to organize your thoughts and sort through what appears to be a mountain of information that you wish to express about your topic, you have to tackle the problem of how to best organize all this information. Four common methods of organizing body paragraphs are listed here.

- Work chronologically

  This type of structure works well for essays in which time sequence or chronology matters. If you are writing about the evolution of breast cancer treatment, it would make sense to begin with older treatments and then work up to more modern ones.

- Work climactically

  Like the long distance runner who chooses to start a marathon slowly in order to conserve energy for a strong finish, authors often choose to end their essays with what they determine to be their strongest point in order to leave a memorable impression on the reader.

- Work spatially

  Sometimes it is effective to organize an essay spatially. For example, if you are contrasting diabetes patterns in the three continents of Africa, Asia and North America, it would make sense to work either geographically eastwards or geographically westwards. The author could begin with a discussion of diabetes in North America, move eastward to Africa, and then further eastward to Asia.

- Work randomly

  Sometimes body organization is nothing more than authorial preference. If there is no apparent pattern to your points and no perceived advantage in organizing according to a theme or pattern, the random ordering of main points is acceptable.

DON'T

- Don't include material in your essay's body that does not aid you in your argument or that does not support your thesis.
- Don't repeat information in the different body paragraphs.

TRY IT YOURSELF

1. Suppose you are writing a five-paragraph essay based on each of the thesis statements below. What would your three topic sentences be for each thesis statement?

   a) The advantages of computerized record-keeping in hospitals include efficiency, accuracy, and service enhancement.
   b) The patient-client relationship is centred on trust, patience, and responsibility.
   c) Better education as to what constitutes an emergency, an increase in the number of emergency rooms, and presence of more trained hospital staff can help decrease waiting times in Toronto emergency rooms.
   d) The Bachelor of Nursing degree is intense, educational, and marketable.
   e) Elder abuse, improperly trained personnel, and overworked staff are three rampant problems in Canadian nursing homes.

Conclusion

The last paragraph of your essay is your conclusion. It is the last part of the essay that your reader sees, so it should leave a memorable impression. The first sentence of your conclusion is known as a **summary statement** and restates (not copies) your thesis. The summary statement signals closure for the reader.

DON'T

- Don't introduce new ideas or new arguments in the conclusion.

> *Over the course of your education, you will be required to write several essays. Why do you think the essay is such a crucial component of your program? List five skills that are developed during the process of writing an essay. For each, list one reason that this skill is valuable in your chosen field.*

WRITING IN AN ACADEMIC SETTING

The essay "Dangers of Online Medical Advice" (Box 3.9) in its original form is a five-paragraph essay. In the revision below, however, it has been written as one long paragraph. See if you can find the starting and end points for the various essay sections that have been discussed so far.

BOX 3.9   Dangers of Online Medical Advice

By Mari Flores

A quick online search for "online medical advice" generates 198 million results. The various sites offer medical advice for all types of medical conditions and make it easy for people to understand complicated medical jargon by oversimplifying the information. They even cross-reference symptoms to other related conditions so people can pinpoint with more accuracy what they are suffering from. Despite these attempts, online medical advice is dangerous because it is misleading, the medical advice is not certified, and people may follow dangerous recommendations. Online medical advice misleads readers. Most of the information posted on the sites is very general. Medical conditions are cross-referenced when symptoms are common, and the list of what a person may be suffering from becomes long and complicated. People seeking online medical help may be under stress or fear that they have a serious condition and fall in the information overload trap. They fail to realize that one size does not fit all. Readers may accept the advice without questioning the implications of such action. Other people may be increasing their anxiety and stress by feeding into their minds the idea that they suffer from a severe medical condition. An online doctor cannot possibly diagnose any one person accurately without being able to go beyond superficial questions. The online doctor does not know the medical history of the patient, nor is the patient physically present in order to make an accurate assessment. Also, many sites present ads for drugs that people can access directly from the manufacturers. Without verifying the authenticity and true medical background of these advice givers, readers cannot ascertain they are receiving real medical advice. Online doctors or medical advice may not even be from certified health care professionals. Anyone can post information on the Internet. Medical advice sites can take the form of forums or blogs where people share their symptoms, conditions, home remedies, medical woes, and stories of how they triumphed over their illness, and they even suggest what medication to take. However, they are not health care professionals. Without the assurance that a person is dealing with a licenced professional, it is best not to seek medical advice from any source other than a certified physician, in person. People may follow dangerous medical recommendations obtained from online sites. If patients fear the life-threatening condition they have narrowed down their symptoms to, they will try their best to mitigate their anxiety by trying anything. If a forum participant recommended a particular drug, the patient may try it, or he or she may try untested alternative medicine instead of seeking professional medical treatments. Patients who seek medical assistance even for the smallest of symptoms can easily be trapped by online medical advice into taking the information and overcomplicating their need to find a solution to their condition. Patients could purchase medication online, or they may put undue pressure on their family doctor to prescribe the drugs they read about online without thinking of the potential side effects or interaction with their existing medication. People could easily fall for the promises given and self-treat their condition without thinking about the side effects of the medication. Following medical recommendations from unknown online sources is a risky venture. Medical advice should be an in-person activity with a health care professional. Online medical advice can be dangerous because it can be misleading, the medical help offered is not verifiable, and the recommendations presented may cause more harm than good. The Internet offers vast amounts of information that can be helpful in many ways, but those feeling ill or suffering from medical symptoms they are not certain about are better served by seeking immediate medical help in a hospital or from their own health care practitioner.

Source: Adapted from "Dangers of online medical advice," by Mari Flores. Reprinted with permission.

The thesis statement is

_____

The topic sentence of the first paragraph is

_____

The topic sentence of the second paragraph is

_____

The topic sentence of the third paragraph is

_____

The topic sentence of the fourth paragraph is

_____

The summary statement is

_____

THE ACADEMIC REPORT

As mentioned previously, there is no "one size fits all" model for either the essay or the academic report: report organization and content depend on the requirements of a particular discipline, course, and instructor.

In preparing an academic report, you may be asked to conduct **primary research**, where you conduct your own study or experiment, and then present your findings; or you may be asked to do **secondary research**, where you analyze and interpret the research of others. Below you will find definitions and explanations for common report sections. Your instructor will tell you which sections he or she wants you to incorporate.

Abstract

The abstract appears after the **title page** (see page 91) and is a brief summary of the major points of your report. As the abstract summarizes your report, it allows a reader to quickly determine whether to read further or not. The abstract follows the title page and appears on a page by itself. It is a maximum of 120 words long and is written in block (not indented) format. Even though the abstract is one of the first report sections the reader sees, it is often the last thing written.

Introduction

This section outlines the purpose and scope of your study, experiment, or analysis. Whether your report is based on a study or experiment, or you are writing an informational piece, you must have a **purpose statement** or **objective**: a clear and focused goal that is articulated at the outset of the report. The purpose statement in a report serves the same function as a thesis in an essay: it tells the reader what the purpose or goal of the report is. Like the thesis statement, it should be clear and focused, and express the report's contents.

Review of Literature

A literature review appears at the beginning of a report and summarizes and evaluates the significant literature that you have looked at in preparing your report. You do not have to include all the sources that you have read; rather, the sources you choose for comment should be organized around the central purpose of your paper. Ultimately, a good literature review shows that the author has done comprehensive background reading and research on his or her topic; as well, the review provides context for the information and research that are to come.

Materials and Method

If your report is based on primary research, you will need to include a Materials and Method section. Here, you describe the set-up of your study and the techniques you used to acquire the data contained in your report. Methods of experimentation and data collection are discipline-specific, so will vary, but commonly include questionnaires, interviews, focus groups, and similar tools. Your description of the materials and methods used in your study must be detailed and comprehensive.

Results

This section details the presentation of your findings. It is important to note that the data you present here should be stated objectively and should not be commented on or analyzed.

Discussion

In this section, you interpret and comment on the findings presented in the Results section. The Discussion section is the place to comment on notable patterns or relationships that connect to your original purpose or objective. Additionally, you should connect your personal findings to any existing research. Any problems with or gaps in your methods and/or materials should also be commented on, and recommendations for further research should be made.

References

This section details the sources that you have paraphrased, summarized, or quoted in your report and appears at the end of your document. Entries are double-spaced and listed alphabetically according to the last name of the author. Books, magazines, and websites are all cited differently (see page 94). The first line of each entry begins at the left-hand margin; second and subsequent lines are indented five to seven spaces.

Tables

Tables should be placed after the References section. Each table should be on its own page. Make sure that your tables are labelled consecutively and you follow correct rules for formatting captions (see page 95).

Figure Captions

The Figure Captions page follows any tables and lists all the captions for the figures used in your report (see page 96).

Figures

Any figures you have used should be placed after the Figure Captions page. Each figure should be placed on a separate page.

Appendix

Some reports also include an Appendix. This section follows the References section, and any tables and figures. An Appendix contains material that is referred to in the text of the report but has been determined to be distracting, awkward, or too verbose to be placed within the main text. Your Appendix should include only those items that enhance your report's message. Common items found in an Appendix include questionnaires, statistical data, or detailed description. Tables and figures that appear as part of an appendix are numbered separately from those belonging to the main text; the table or figure number is preceded by the letter of the appendix (e.g., Appendix A might include Table A1 and Figures A1 and A2).

HEADINGS

Headings help with the organization of information and determine the hierarchy of information in your report. The number of heading levels used depends on the number of categories and sub-categories in your report. The sixth edition of the APA manual stresses the following five-level heading structure:

Level 1: **Centred, Bold, Standard Capitalization**

Level 2: **Flush Left, Bold, Standard Capitalization**

Level 3: **Indented, bold, lowercase, period at the end.** There is no hard return after the heading; the first line of the paragraph follows the period at the end of the header.

Level 4: ***Indented, bold, italicized, lowercase, period at the end.*** There is no hard return after the heading; the first line of the paragraph follows the period.

Level 5: *Indented, italicized, lowercase, period at the end.* There is no hard return after the heading; the first line of the paragraph follows the period.

Most papers at an undergraduate level will not require more than three different heading levels. In order to incorporate headings correctly, you must first determine how many different heading levels you will need. Once you have done this, follow the guidelines below:

- If you have one level of title, use Level 1 only.
- If you have two levels of titles, use Levels 1 and 2.
- If you have three levels of titles, use Levels 1, 2, and 3.
- If you have four levels of titles, use Levels 1, 2, 3, and 4.
- If you have five levels of titles, use Levels 1, 2, 3, 4, and 5.

USING VISUALS IN YOUR REPORT

Visuals in reports can be greatly beneficial. They concentrate information and allow complex ideas to be expressed creatively and efficiently. According to APA conventions, visuals are divided into two categories: tables and figures. Tables are instantly recognizable by rows and columns that contain either numerical data or text (matrix). A figure, in contrast, refers to any type of visual that is not a table. This includes graphs, charts, drawings, and photographs.

APA Standards for Both Figures and Tables

According to APA guidelines, when using visuals in academic reports, you should follow the standards below:

- Any visual used must be referred to in your text.
- Figures should complement, rather than duplicate, textual information.
- All figures and tables are numbered consecutively with Arabic numerals (e.g., Figure 1, Figure 2, Table 1, Table 2). Titles of tables appear at the top of the table; figure captions appear below the figure.
- You must cite the source for your visual in a source note below your table or after the caption below your figure. Here are two examples:

For a visual from a journal article:

Source: From "Insulin dependency in juvenile-onset diabetics," by E. Singer & Z. M. Hallikainen, 2007, *Journal of Diabetic Research, 45,* p. 739. Copyright [year] by [the name of the copyright holder]. Reprinted [or adapted] with permission.

For a visual from a book:

Source: Adapted from *Ideas about learning and memory*, by J. R. Smith, 2012, p. 34, Yellowknife: University of the Northwest Territories Press. Copyright [year] by [the name of the copyright holder]. Reprinted [or adapted] with permission.

- A citation for the source of any visuals that come from other sources should also appear on your References page (see p. 94).
- Manuscript style dictates that visuals should be placed at the end of the report (after the References page but before the Appendix). Each table and figure is placed on a separate page; a Figure Captions page, which lists the captions of all the figures used, precedes the figures section.
- Figure and table placement in undergraduate or non-published works depends on instructor preference. Your professor may require that a visual be

placed on a separate page immediately following its first reference or that it be directly incorporated into the body of the essay or report.

Figure Captioning: The Specifics

- The word *Figure* and its respective number should be italicized with a period after it.
- Capitalize only first words and proper nouns in figure captions, and end the caption with a period. The source information follows the figure caption.
- Unlike table titles, which are placed above a table, figure captions appear below the figure. They are also listed on a separate page, in a list of Figure Captions, as explained on pp. 96–97.

FIGURE 3.1 | **Sample Figure and Caption**

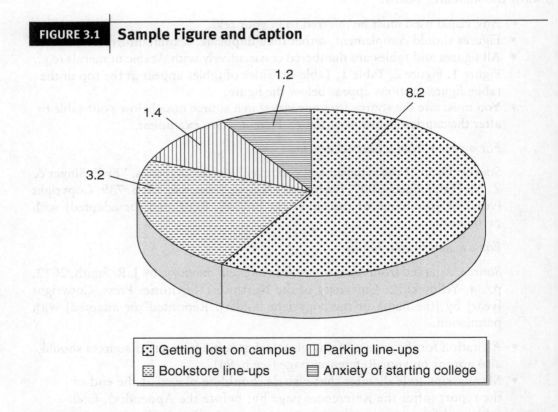

Figure 1. Top four frustrations as reported by a random sampling of Lester College students the first week of classes. From "College students: Behaviours," by L. Ross, 2006, *Journal of Post-Secondary Education, 13*, p. 86. Copyright 2006 by L. Ross.

Table Titles: The Specifics

- The word *Table*, along with its respective number, appears on a line by itself. The table title is italicized with standard capitalization (see p. 95). The entire title is placed above the visual. A double space separates the table heading from the table title. See example below.

TABLE 3.2 **Sample Table and Caption**

Table 6

A Sample Food Diary Template From Sunflower Health Clinic

Day	Breakfast	Lunch	Dinner	Snack
Sunday				
Monday				
Tuesday				
Wednesday				
Thursday				
Friday				
Saturday				

Source: From "Tracking nutrition," by J. Edgell, 2007, *Dietician Quarterly,* 2, p. 320. Copyright 2007 by J. Edgell.

SAMPLE STUDENT APA REPORT

In the sample student report that follows (Box 3.10), excerpts from a much longer report have been used to model many of the APA formalities introduced in this chapter. Specifically, the model paper demonstrates proper formatting of the following key sections: title page, Abstract, tables and figures sections, as well as the References page. Additionally, the sample text pages model correct APA style headings and block quotation formatting, as well as figure and table captioning.

| BOX 3.10 | **Sample Student Report (Excerpt)** |

Running head: CAUSES OF HEARING LOSS   1

> The running head is identified on the title page, which is also page 1; page number appears at the top right on the same line.

The Causes of Hearing Loss

Erlinda S. Taruc

GASA 200 (Writing for the Sciences I)

Prof. Sobia Zaman

November 30, 2012

> The report title, author, course, professor, and date of submission should be double-spaced and centred on the title page.

Source: Courtesy of Erlinda Taruc

Abstract

Hearing is a sense through which a person experiences the world he or she lives in. Reduction or complete loss of sensitivity to sound, however, can greatly affect and limit a person's participation in daily activities. Consequently, knowing the source of one's hearing problem is essential to one's well-being. Causes of hearing loss vary and are often dependant on time of onset, severity, and age. When attempting to categorize the causes of hearing loss, the origins of the loss must be taken into consideration. This informative report explains causes of hearing loss originating from external, middle, or inner ear damage. Hearing loss that originates in these three areas is classified as conductive, sensorineural, or mixed.

The running head is placed one inch from the top of the page and flush left. Page number appears top right.

The Abstract should not exceed 120 words in length. It should summarize the main points of your research. The Abstract should be written in block format [not indented], and appears on a page by itself.

continued

Conductive Hearing Loss (CHL)

Hearing disorders that affect the outer and middle ear are termed conductive hearing loss. CHL arises when a blockage, physical defect, or damage to these structures prevents sound from reaching the inner ear. The external auditory canal may be blocked, the three tiny bones of the middle ear may fail to conduct sound to the cochlea, or the eardrum may fail to vibrate in response to sound. These problems may be corrected by medical or surgical interventions (Burkey, 2003). Figure 1 illustrates an overview of the human ear.

Causes of Conductive Hearing Loss

Some of the possible causes of conductive hearing loss include a lodged object in the ear canal, excessive amount of wax blocking the ear canal, infection in the outer or middle ear cavity, puncturing of the eardrum, disconnection of the middle ear bones, and deformity of the outer or middle ear.

Foreign bodies in the external auditory canal. Children sometimes push small bits and pieces, such as pebbles, bugs, beads, toy parts, cereals, and other food particles into their ear canals. The obstruction can result in discomfort, aches, infection, or hearing loss (Cole & Flexer, 2007).

Cerumen or earwax impaction. This condition occurs when there is an excessive amount of earwax or cerumen that blocks the ear canal. Cerumen is a typical body secretion found along the skin of the ear canal of the outer ear. Earwax protects the auditory canal by discouraging dust and other airborne particles from entering and getting too deep into the canal, which can eventually lead to hearing impairment (Isaacson & Vora, 2003). Marcincuk and Roland (2002) further elaborated:

> Exostoses occur when the external canal is repeatedly exposed to cold air or water. Cold exposure irritates the periosteum [connective tissue membrane that surrounds all bones except those at joints] and stimulates bony growth.... Osteomas are benign neoplasms [tumors] of the bone. They are less common than exostoses and are usually single and unilateral [hearing loss in one ear]. (p. 84)

Quotations longer than 40 words are set off as block quotations. Notice, in block quotations, that the final period is placed before the bracketed source information.

Sensorineural Hearing Loss (SNHL)

When a hearing loss results from disorders in the inner ear, it is referred to as sensorineural hearing loss. The damage is usually in the cochlea, which contains numerous microscopic sensory receptors called hair cells. These inner hair cells convert sound vibrations into electrical signals that travel as nerve impulses to the brain, where their meanings are processed and interpreted. Problems in the auditory nerves, which send sound to the brain, also contribute to SNHL (Burkey, 2003). Table 1 defines various degrees of hearing loss, including sensorineural loss.

Accordingly, Tang, Montemayor, and Pereira (2006) stated, "Many hearing disorders involve irreversible damage to hair cells and their associated nerves and result in permanent hearing impairment ... known as sensorineural hearing loss" (p. 525). SNHL can affect the clarity of hearing and volume of sound, so even if sound is loud enough to be perceived, substantial sound distortion can occur, which results in difficulty understanding speech (Hewitt & Wareing, 2006).

continued

References

Burkey, J. M. (2003). *Overcoming hearing aid fears: The road to better hearing.* New Jersey: Rutgers.

Canadian Academy of Audiology. (2006). *How do we hear?* Retrieved from http://www.canadianaudiology.ca/consumers/children/index.html

Canadian Hearing Instrument Practitioners Society. (2004). *Canadian consumer guide to hearing loss and hearing aids*. Retrieved from http://www.hearingloss.ca/pdf/Consumer%20Guide-Hearing%20Loss%20and%20Hearing%20Aids.pdf

Cole, E. B., & Flexer, C. (2007). *Children with hearing loss: Developing listening and talking*. San Diego: Plural.

Isaacson, J., & Vora, N. (2003, September 15). Differential diagnosis and treatment of hearing loss. *American Family Physician, 68*(6), 1125–1132.

Marcincuk, M., & Roland, P. (2002, April). Geriatric hearing loss: Understanding the causes and providing appropriate treatment. *Geriatrics, 57*(4), 44–59.

Miller, M., & Schein, J. (2005, July). Selected complex auditory disorders. *Journal of Rehabilitation Research & Development, 42,* 1–8.

Newton, V., & Vallely, P. (Eds.). (2006). Infection and hearing impairment. West Sussex: Whurr.

Subha, S., & Raman, R. (2006). Role of impacted cerumen in hearing loss. *ENT: Ear, Nose & Throat Journal, 85*(10), 650–653.

Tang, L., Montemayor, C., & Pereira, F. (2006, September). Sensorineural hearing loss: Potential therapies and gene targets for drug development. *IUBMB Life, 58*(9), 525–530.

Table 1

Degree of Hearing Loss

Place tables after the References section. Tables should be titled as shown (see p. 89.)

Hearing Threshold	Description of Hearing
0 dB	Perfect
1 – 25 dB	Normal
26 – 40 dB	Mild Loss
41 – 55 dB	Moderate Loss
56 – 80 dB	Severe Loss
81+ dB	Profound Loss

Source: Adapted from *Canadian Consumer Guide to Hearing Loss and Hearing Aids* (p. 4), by Canadian Hearing Instrument Practitioners Society, 2004. Retrieved from http://www.hearingloss.ca/pdf/Consumer%20Guide-Hearing%20Loss%20and%20Hearing%20Aids.pdf

continued

List figure captions on a separate page and format as shown. Complete figure captioning instructions are provided on pp. 87–88.

Figure Captions

Figure 1. The anatomy of the human ear.

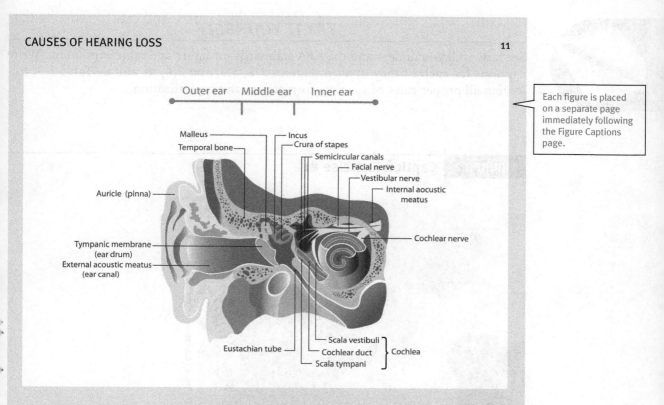

Outer ear   Middle ear   Inner ear

Malleus
Temporal bone
Incus
Crura of stapes
Semicircular canals
Facial nerve
Vestibular nerve
Internal aocustic
meatus

Auricle (pinna)

Cochlear nerve

Tympanic membrane
(ear drum)
External acoustic meatus
(ear canal)

Eustachian tube
Scala vestibuli
Cochlear duct   Cochlea
Scala tympani

Each figure is placed
on a separate page
immediately following
the Figure Captions
page.

Figure 1. The anatomy of the human ear. From *How do we hear?*, by Canadian
Academy of Audiology, 2006. Retrieved from http://www.canadianaudiology.ca/
consumers/children/index.html. Copyright 2006 by the Canadian Academy of
Audiology.

Source: From "The causes of hearing loss," by Erlinda S. Taruc, 2012, November. Courtesy of Erlinda Taruc.

TRY IT YOURSELF

See how well you understand the APA standards for figure and table captioning. Write captions for each of the visuals in Figures 3.2, 3.3, and 3.4, as well as Table 3.3, following all proper rules of spacing, formatting, and capitalization.

| FIGURE 3.2 | Caption Exercise #1 |

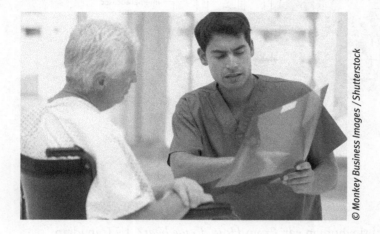

© Monkey Business Images / Shutterstock

| FIGURE 3.3 | Caption Exercise #2 |

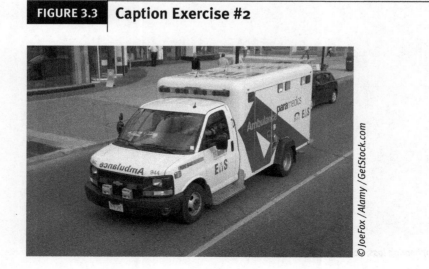

© JoeFox / Alamy / GetStock.com

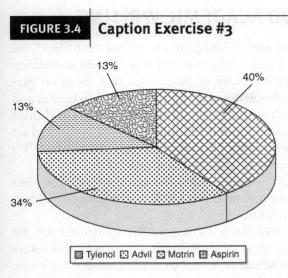

Legend:
- ⊠ Tylenol
- ⊡ Advil
- ⊟ Motrin
- ⊞ Aspirin

TABLE 3.3 | **Caption Exercise #4**

NUMBER	SQUARE	CUBE	SQUARE ROOT OF NUMBER
1	1	1	1.000
2	4	8	1.414
3	9	27	1.732
4	16	64	2.000
5	25	125	2.236
6	36	216	2.449
7	49	343	2.645
8	64	512	2.828
9	81	729	3.000
10	100	1000	3.162
11	121	1331	3.316
12	144	1728	3.464
13	169	2197	3.605
14	196	2744	3.741

CHARACTERISTICS OF GOOD ACADEMIC WRITING

Write in CLEAR language. For summaries and critical analyses, do not "translate" the original document word for word with a thesaurus; you will end up with something that does not make sense, and you may be guilty of plagiarism (for more on plagiarism, please see Chapter 4). For all academic documents, avoid technical jargon and use words that you are familiar with. Don't try to sound "smart"—it always backfires!

Be OBJECTIVE. Any opinions expressed in academic writing must be backed up by facts. Don't rely on your "feelings" or "beliefs." Use the first-person singular ("I") sparingly, and avoid it completely in summaries and academic reports.

Academic writing should be CONCISE. Include the necessary information, but edit out unnecessary details, digressions, or information that does not directly support your thesis or serve the purpose of the document.

Academic writing should be ORGANIZED according to the guidelines for the specific type of document. Whichever method of organization you use, make sure that the ideas proceed logically. Ask a classmate or friend to read through your essay, report, summary, or analysis to ensure that the document is easy to follow.

Provide the reader with ACCURATE information; do your research carefully and double-check facts when possible.

As always, proofread all written documents to ensure CORRECT grammar, spelling, and punctuation. A grammatical error or confused word can undermine your credibility; your reader may assume that you are careless and therefore not a reliable source of information.

Be sure that your writing is AUDIENCE-APPROPRIATE; if it is aimed at a general audience, do not use overly technical or specialized vocabulary. Define any unfamiliar terms.

Academic writing must be THOROUGH. In a summary or analysis, do not miss any of the original's main points. In an essay or report, cover all sides of an argument and/or provide all relevant information. Be sure to document all sources using APA guidelines, which will be discussed in the next chapter.

CHAPTER LINKS FOR FURTHER EXPLORATION

- OWL at Purdue (http://owl.english.purdue.edu/owl/resource/560/01)

Purdue University's Online Writing Lab is an excellent source of detailed information on APA formatting guidelines.

- The University of Toronto's Writing Centre (http://www.writing.utoronto.ca/advice)

This site provides useful advice on writing academic papers.

CHAPTER 4

FINDING, INCORPORATING, AND CITING SOURCES

At the end of this chapter, you should be able to

- find appropriate academic articles to use as sources in your writing assignments
- distinguish between paraphrasing and plagiarism, and incorporate paraphrasing into your writing
- understand the reasons for avoiding plagiarism and know how to avoid it correctly document sources using APA guidelines

FINDING SOURCES

Locating information about a topic is an essential skill for both postsecondary education and your future career. While many students assume that the task of conducting research has been made easier by the proliferation of online encyclopedias, websites, and other online sources, it has actually been made more difficult. With an endless supply of information available, sorting out the useful, relevant, reliable sources of information from the rest can be an overwhelming task.

The Pitfalls of Google

Many students begin their research by typing their topic into Google or another search engine. Say you were asked to write a report classifying the various treatments for endometriosis. If you were to type "endometriosis" into a search engine, at time of publication, the search would yield 11,400,000 results; the top three results are 1) a Wikipedia entry, 2) an overview on the disease published by the Mayo Clinic, and 3) a general article on medicine.net. If you were to attempt to refine your search by typing in "endometriosis treatment," the results would narrow to 8,620,000, with the same three results within the top five. All of these are broad encyclopedia or fact-sheet style sources of general information. Scanning through the top ten results of both searches, we did not find a single article that would be a useful, relevant, reliable source for our hypothetical assignment.

If Google and other general search engines cast too wide a net and don't turn up the right type of article, what should you do? There are several options:

1. Your **college or university library** provides access to databases of articles and other resources, listed by subject area. These are searchable online, and many of the articles are available in full text, which means they can be read online or printed from your home computer. This is the best place to search. If you require help, ask a librarian or your instructor.

2. **Google Scholar** (scholar.google.com, or select Scholar from the main Google page) limits the search to peer-reviewed articles, dissertations, and books from cross-disciplinary academic sources. Do not simply enter your topic into Google or a similar search engine. Be sure to limit the choice to scholarly articles.

3. Similarly, **Academic Info** (academicinfo.net) is an online education resource centre that features a directory of links and resources arranged by subject area. According to the main page, the resources are compiled "taking into account their accessibility, authoritative sources as well as their ease of use, and aim to present a fair and well-rounded perspective of the respective subject matter."

Why Does My Instructor Discourage the Use of Wikipedia?

Have you had the Wikipedia discussion with your professor yet? When asked to find sources for an academic paper, many students will automatically consult Wikipedia, which is usually within the top five results of a general Google search. Yet professors will tell you that Wikipedia is not an acceptable source for academic papers. Do you know why this is?

1. Wikipedia offers no guarantee of accuracy. A **wiki** is a website that anyone can contribute to or change. A site like Wikipedia is made up of millions of user-created, user-edited entries on an enormous range of topics. While the diversity of contributors does lead to a wide array of articles, and while the ability to edit others' contributions does mean that many inaccuracies are corrected, there is

no formal mechanism for quality control, unlike the factors that guarantee the content in peer-reviewed journals.

2. The articles are general overviews, as in a traditional encyclopedia, and as such are not an appropriate source for specialized research or critical scholarship. Before Wikipedia, most families had access to a set of hardcover encyclopedias. Unlike Wikipedia, they took up a lot of space, were heavy and awkward to access, and could not be updated without replacing the whole set. However, the basic content was the same: summaries of information intended for a general readership. They were not acceptable sources for academic writing either. Your professor will likely require you to use "peer-reviewed" sources, to ensure that your conclusions are based on current, reliable data.

Please note that we are not suggesting that you avoid consulting Wikipedia altogether. It can provide a very useful starting point, as you will see in "Step One" of "The Research Process, Step by Step," below. However, it is a source of general knowledge only, and should not be used to support your argument.

Choose a topic and look it up on Wikipedia. What are some of the reasons that the Wikipedia article would not be an appropriate resource for an academic paper? What types of information are missing from the article? Now, search your library's website for a scholarly article on the same topic. What are the differences between the Wikipedia article and the scholarly article?

What Does *Peer-Reviewed* Mean?

Peer review is a term for a selection process whereby articles are screened by experts in the field (professional "peers" of the article's author). If you were to submit an article about juvenile diabetes to a peer-reviewed journal, your entry would be read by one or more people with a proven research record on similar subjects. If they found your research to be academically credible, the article would be published and future researchers would be able to consult it. If your article contained inaccuracies or faulty reasoning, or was otherwise poorly written, it would not be published. You might say that an article in a peer-reviewed journal has been pre-approved by experts.

How Can You Tell If an Article Is Peer Reviewed?

1. Some databases allow you to limit your search to peer-reviewed articles. On the search form, check a box that says "limit to articles from scholarly publications" or something similar.

2. If you click on the journal title in your database, it should tell you whether the journal is peer-reviewed.

3. Look up the journal online. If the journal is peer-reviewed, its webpage should state this upfront.

Here are some questions you can ask yourself to determine whether a source is trustworthy. Remember, if your source isn't credible, your argument won't be, either.

1. What are the **author's qualifications and affiliations?** What makes him or her an authority on the subject? Is he or she biased? For example, an article on treatments for insomnia, written by the inventor of a new type of pillow for insomniacs, is not an objective source. Look for authors with academic qualifications, such as advanced degrees (MA, MSc, PhD, MD), as well as affiliations with a university or college.

2. What is the **sponsoring organization** for the site? Is it a reputable organization? Is any bias evident in the material? Is the site peer-reviewed? The site's domain is often a clue to its affiliation: *.edu* indicates an educational institution, *.gov* indicates a government organization, and *.org* usually indicates a non-profit or non-commercial organization.

3. What is the **author's purpose** in writing? To inform? To persuade? To promote a product?

4. Does the site contain **current information?** How recently was the site updated? Are the links functional?

5. Are the sources on the site **properly documented?** Is there a list of works cited or references?

TRY IT YOURSELF

Which of these two articles would more useful in preparing an academic report or essay? Why? Even without reading the articles, how can you tell which one is a scholarly article and which one is written for a general readership? List as many reasons as you can.

1. "Assessing Fitness to Drive: Practical Tips for Using the Right Screening Tools for Your Practice," by Bruce Weaver, MSc, and Michel Bedard, PhD. Published in *Canadian Geriatrics Society Journal of CME*, Volume 2, Issue 3, 2012.

2. "Going Off-Road: Should Elderly Drivers Be Subject to Special Testing? Seniors Protest a Move to Standardized Tests That Could Take Away Their Licences," by Peter Shawn Taylor. Published in *Maclean's*, April 4, 2013.

THE RESEARCH PROCESS, STEP BY STEP

Your instructor has assigned you a research paper. The topic: Compare and contrast two similar chronic health conditions, their symptoms, and treatment options.

Step One

This is a very broad topic, so the first step is to narrow it down. What type of conditions would you like to learn more about? Perhaps you are interested in asthma, which is a chronic lung condition. Because you are asked to both compare and contrast, you need to find another chronic lung condition that has both similarities to (compare) and differences from (contrast) asthma. As we indicated above, Wikipedia can be a useful starting point for narrowing down the topic.

Wikipedia has no entries for "chronic lung conditions"; however, at the bottom of the Wikipedia entry on asthma is a section on "Differential Diagnosis" which mentions two conditions—chronic obstructive pulmonary disease (COPD) and pulmonary aspiration—that closely resemble asthma. This gives you somewhere to begin.

Step Two

Once you have narrowed down the topic enough to research further, it is time to search some reputable academic search engines, and to look at some of the resources available through your institution's library.

A search for "asthma or COPD" on Academic Info leads to the database MEDLINEplus, which informs readers of its objectivity: "There is no advertising on this site, nor does it endorse any company or product." The first five results include an article on the coexistence of asthma and COPD, published by the American Academy of Allergy, Asthma, and Immunology, and articles on the diagnosis and treatment of COPD and asthma, published by the National Lung Health Education Program. A search on Google Scholar brings up an article from the peer-reviewed journal *Chest*, by Peter J. Barnes of the Department of Thoracic Medicine, National Heart and Lung Institute, London, UK, entitled "Mechanisms in COPD—Differences From Asthma." A couple of clicks confirm that *Chest* is the official journal of the American College of Chest Physicians and is the leading cardiopulmonary and critical care journal in the world. Add "Canada" to the search string and more articles, including many from *Chest*, appear, including "Asthma Education: The Canadian Experience." The library home page of a typical college library provides links to a number of useful databases, including Academic Search Premier, ProQuest Nursing & Allied Health Source, Health Source: Nursing/Academic Edition, CINAHL (Cumulative Index to Nursing and Health Literature), and MEDLINEplus. Searches for "asthma and treatment or symptoms," and "chronic obstructive pulmonary disease or COPD and treatment or symptoms" result in many useful articles from books and refereed journals.

Step Three

Now that you have located your sources, it is time to read them, looking for information that will support the claims that you are making in your essay or report. Keep a notebook or electronic file for keeping track of relevant quotations and examples to use. Be sure to write down the information about each source, including the page number, in order to make it easy for you to document your sources.

1. Choose one of the following terms and research it on (a) Google, (b) Wikipedia, (c) Google Scholar, and (d) a database subscribed to by your college or university. Compare the results and evaluate their appropriateness as resources for a research essay or report.

Autism Spectrum Disorder	peptic ulcers	midwife
ADHD	echinacea	plantar wart

PLAGIARISM

Plagiarism is the most common form of academic misconduct, and every institution has its own definition of and official policy for dealing with plagiarism. Generally, though, plagiarism is understood as the act of knowingly submitting someone else's work as your own. To avoid plagiarism, you must acknowledge the sources of any ideas, words, or phrases that you use in your writing.

Why Is Plagiarism Wrong?

1. Plagiarism is fraud. By copying someone's ideas and passing them off as your own, you are cheating that person out of his or her intellectual property.

2. You are also demonstrating that you are unable to do the work required for the assigned task and that you lack the ability to think for yourself.

3. Perhaps most importantly, plagiarism can be dangerous in health-related fields; if you prepare a report using data you have hastily copied without checking, you may be spreading false information that may harm patients' health.

4. Finally, you are leaving yourself open to legal action and limiting your employment possibilities.

Imagine that you spent months of hard work on a project, and that you are very proud of the outcome. How would you feel if a coworker passed the work off as hers, and took all the credit for your efforts?

What Is the Difference Between Summarizing or Paraphrasing and Plagiarizing?

A summary or paraphrase of someone else's work changes the wording and structure of the original piece, and includes a citation. Without the citation or mention of the original's author, a summary or paraphrase is plagiarism and is punishable by academic penalty.

Let's look at three different ways to incorporate a source into your writing:

Original

Sometimes, humans and animals can pass strains of flu back and forth to one another through direct close contact. When a swine influenza virus does affect a human, there is also a risk that the animal influenza can mutate and then spread directly between humans. More investigation is needed on how easily the virus spreads between people, but it is believed that it is spread the same way as regular seasonal influenza. Influenza and other respiratory infections are transmitted from person to person when germs enter the nose and/or throat.

Source: From "Fact sheet H1N1 flu virus (human swine flu)," by Public Health Agency of Canada, 2009. Retrieved from http://www.phac-aspc.gc.ca/alert-alerte/swine-porcine/fs-fr_swine-eng.php

Version #1

It is possible for humans and animals to pass the flu to one another through direct contact. When a human contracts the swine flu virus, the animal influenza can mutate and spread directly between humans. There needs to be more research done into how easily the virus spreads between people, but it is believed that it is spread when germs enter the nose or throat, the same way as the regular flu.

Do you think this is plagiarism? Let's look at the two passages sentence by sentence:

Original: Sometimes, humans and animals can pass strains of flu back and forth to one another through direct close contact.

Version #1: It is possible for humans and animals to pass the flu to one another through direct contact.

Original: When a swine influenza virus does affect a human, there is also a risk that the animal influenza can mutate and then spread directly between humans.

Version #1: When a human contracts the swine flu virus, the animal influenza can mutate and spread directly between humans.

Original: More investigation is needed on how easily the virus spreads between people, but it is believed that it is spread the same way as regular seasonal influenza. Influenza and other respiratory infections are transmitted from person to person when germs enter the nose and/or throat.

Version #1: There needs to be more research done into how easily the virus spreads between people, but it is believed that it is spread when germs enter the nose or throat, the same way as the regular flu.

Is there a significant difference between the original and Version #1? Where does the information in Version #1 come from? If a student were to include these sentences in an essay or report, would they represent that student's original thought? Remember, you must cite anything in your writing that comes from somewhere else, even if the words have been changed.

Version #1 is an example of plagiarism. A student handing it in would receive a grade of 0 and may face further academic penalty.

The student could have avoided plagiarism by referring the source of the material, as seen in Version #2, below. Keep in mind that the source needs to be given every time paraphrased material is used.

Version #2

According to the Public Health Agency of Canada's *Fact Sheet for the H1N1 Flu Virus* (2009), it is possible for humans and animals to pass strains of influenza to one another. It is also possible for animal influenza to mutate and then pass from human to human. While further investigation is needed to determine how H1N1 is spread among humans, it is believed that, as with regular seasonal influenza, it is spread through germs entering the respiratory tract.

Version #2 is a paraphrase; while the ideas come from somewhere else, the student has changed the wording and the order of the ideas. This is not plagiarism. When the exact wording of the original is used, use quotation marks, as in Version # 3, below.

Version #3

According to the Public Health Agency of Canada's *Fact Sheet for the H1N1 Flu Virus* (2009), it is possible for humans and animals to pass strains of influenza to one another. It is also possible for animal influenza to mutate and then pass from human

I'm dishonest.

I don't mind cheating another person.

I can't do the work myself.

I'm lazy and give up easily.

I can't come up with my own ideas.

I'd rather cut corners than do a thorough job.

I don't take pride in my work.

I can't be trusted.

© Lasse Kristensen / Shutterstock

What does plagiarism say about you?

to human. "There needs to be more research done into how easily the virus spreads between people, but it is believed that it is spread when germs enter the nose or throat, the same way as the regular flu" (Public Health Agency of Canada, 2009).

DOCUMENTING SOURCES IN APA STYLE

When you use sources to support your arguments, you need to document them properly. The two main documentation styles in North America are MLA (Modern Language Association) in the humanities, and APA (American Psychological Association) in the sciences and social sciences. "APA style" refers to the standard academic paper format that is endorsed by the American Psychological Association (APA) and used in the sciences and social sciences. Since 1929, the APA has published a set of guidelines for preparing a scholarly paper; a paper prepared according to these guidelines meets the criteria for consideration for publication in a professional journal in the sciences or social sciences. The APA style conventions for the format of the essay or report were covered in the previous chapter. Documentation in APA style consists of two components: in-text citations and a list of references.

Because the rules for APA documentation are very complex, we will cover only the basic rules and most common student errors. For more detailed information, please consult one of the resources listed at the end of this chapter.

In-Text Citations

The term "in-text citation" refers to a reference that is contained in the body of your essay. When you quote or paraphrase material from an external source, you are required to let the reader know where you obtained the material. Box 4.1 addresses frequently asked questions on APA in-text citations.

BOX 4.1   APA In-text Citations FAQ

1. What do I do if there is no author listed for an article I'm using? What do I do if there's no date listed?

   • When a source has no named author, cite the first few words of the title, followed by the year of publication. Italicize titles of books or reports; put titles of articles in quotation marks. If there is no date listed, use the abbreviation "n.d."

   ("Breathe Easy," 2003)   ("Breathe Easy," n.d.)

continued

---

2. A lot of the sources I'm using have more than one author. Do I need to list all of them?

- For a work with two authors, cite both names every time you refer to the work.

- For a work with three to five authors, cite all the names the first time you refer to the work; for all other references to the work, cite only the first author, followed by "et al." (the abbreviation of *et alia*, which is Latin for "and the others").

- First reference: (Canning, Courage, & Frizzell, 2004)

- All future references: (Canning et al., 2004)

- For a work with six or more authors, cite only the name of the first author, followed by "et al."

- I'm using two sources written by the same author. How do I distinguish between them?

- Include the year of publication in the citation. This will help your reader identify the source. If both sources are published in the same year, use the lower-case letters a, b, c, and so on, to distinguish between them.

   (Barnes, 2003), (Barnes, 2005a), (Barnes 2005b)

3. I'm using an online source and can't find page numbers. What do I do?

- For sources that lack page numbers, use the abbreviation "para." followed by the paragraph number. You could also provide a section heading, plus the paragraph number within the section. Do not use the page numbers of printed web pages.

   (Barnes, 2003, para. 25)

4. My source is published by a group or corporation. Do I proceed as if there were no author listed?

- For documents authored by corporations, government agencies, or other groups or associations, cite the full name of the group in all citations. If the name is long and there is a common abbreviation for it, put the abbreviation in square brackets following the first citation and use only the abbreviation in all subsequent citations.

   (Canadian Pharmacists Association [CPhA], 2013, p. 24)

5. The work I want to cite is a classic and has two publication dates. Which one do I use?

- For works published a long time ago, cite both the date of original publication and the date of your edition. The page number will refer to the edition you are using.

- For *Gray's Anatomy*, originally published in 1858: (Gray, 1858/2008, p. 150)

6. How do I cite a film or television broadcast?

- Follow the same author-date format as for print sources, using the producer, director, and/or writer as the "author," and the release or airing date as the "date."

- For the film *Bringing out the Dead*, directed by Martin Scorsese: (Scorsese, 1999)

Quotations

When you quote material directly from a source within your paper, you need to indicate the source. In APA format, this is done using the author-date-page method; the author's last name, the date of publication, and the page number (if available) must appear in the text, either in the same sentence preceding the quotation, or in parentheses after the quotation.

Examples:

Roy Ashmeade fought the Ontario government for access to Vidaza, which "was the only treatment that held the hope of extending his life after he was diagnosed with myelodysplastic syndrome, which occurs when blood-forming cells in the bone marrow are damaged" (Priest, 2009, A8).

In his 2009 article, Priest documents Roy Ashmeade's fight with the Ontario government for access to Vidaza, which "was the only treatment that held the hope of extending his life after he was diagnosed with myelodysplastic syndrome, which occurs when blood-forming cells in the bone marrow are damaged" (A8).

Note: If there are quotation marks, they should precede the parentheses. Other punctuation (period, comma, etc.) should follow the parentheses.

Paraphrases

A paraphrase is a restatement of the content of a text, using different words. When you are paraphrasing or summarizing material from a source, only the author's name and the date need to be provided.

Example:

Roy Ashmeade, diagnosed with myelodysplastic syndrome, fought the Ontario government for access to Vidaza, a drug that could possibly have prolonged his life (Priest, 2009).

List of References

The in-text citations are intended to direct readers to the more complete list of references at the end of the paper. All sources cited in the paper must appear in the list of references. (See Box 4.2 for answers to frequently asked questions.) Your References list should be double-spaced, and should begin on a separate page, with the title "References" centred at the top of the page. See the sample References list in Box 4.3 (p. 114).

Consult the online sources listed on p. 115 for more detailed instructions.

BOX 4.2   **APA Reference Page FAQ**

1. What do I do if there is no author listed for an article I'm using? What do I do if there's no date listed?

   - If no author is given, begin the entry with the title of the source. List the source alphabetically by the first letter of the first word (not including "a" or "the") of the title.

   Breathe easy: Good nutrition can help keep your lungs healthy. (2003, June). *Environmental Nutrition, 26*(6), 1, 6. Retrieved from http://www .environmentalnutrition.com

   - If no date is given, use the abbreviation "n.d." (for "no date") where the date would be.

   World Health Organization. (n.d.). *International travel and health*. Retrieved from http://www.who.int/ith/en/index.html

2. A lot of the sources I'm using have more than one author. In what order do I list the authors? How do I separate the names?

   - List the authors in the same order that they are listed on the title page of the book or the first page of the article. Do not alphabetize the names. Use an ampersand (&) instead of the word "and" when separating authors' names. For entries with more than two authors, separate the names by commas and place an ampersand before the last name of the last author listed.

   Berlin, L., Albertsson, D., Bengtsson Tops, A., Dahlberg, K., & Grahn, B. (2009, July). Elderly women's experiences of living with fall risk in a fragile body: A reflective lifeworld approach. *Health & Social Care in the Community, 17*(4), 379–387. doi:10.1111/j.1365-2524.2008.00836.x. Epub 2009

3. I'm confused about quotation marks, underlining, and italics. When do I use each one?

   - Italicize titles of longer works (books, encyclopedias, journals, newspapers, movies, etc.).

   - Do not italicize, underline, put quotation marks around, or distinguish in any other way the titles of shorter works (articles, essays, poems, stories, etc.).

   Lewis, S. (2008). Pandemic: My country is on its knees. In K. A. Ackley, G. K. Blank, & S. E. Hume (Eds.), *Perspectives on contemporary issues: Reading across the disciplines* (pp. 274–390). Toronto: Nelson.

   Canning, P. M., Courage, M. L., & Frizzell, L. M. (2004, August 3). Prevalence of overweight and obesity in a provincial population of Canadian preschool children. *CMAJ: Canadian Medical Association Journal, 171*(3), 240–242. doi:10.1503/cmaj.1040075

4. What words do I capitalize?

- Use standard title capitalization for journal and newspaper titles (e.g., *The Canadian Journal of Occupational Therapy*; *The Globe and Mail*): Capitalize all words except conjunctions, articles, and prepositions under 4 letters; capitalize first and last word of title and subtitle regardless of length.

- For other works (books, articles, web pages, etc.), only the following should be capitalized: the first letter of the first word of a title; the first letter of the first word following a colon or a dash in the title; proper nouns (e.g., *Canadian nursing: Issues and perspectives*; Crunch time for public health care in Quebec).

5. How do I cite online sources, including websites and online databases?

- For an article from a website, follow the format for an article in a journal, providing the web address. Follow the same rules for print sources where no author or date is listed. Some articles will list a Digital Object Identifier (DOI) on the first page. If this is provided, you will not need to provide the web address. Simply copy and paste the DOI into your References list.

Iezzoni, L. I., & Ogg, M. (2012). Patient's perspective: Hard lessons from a long hospital stay. *American Journal of Nursing, 112*(4), 39–42. doi:10.1097/01.NAJ.0000413457.53110.3a

- For a journal or magazine article retrieved from a database, if no DOI exists, provide the home page URL of the journal (this sometimes requires a short Internet search).

Breathe easy: Good nutrition can help keep your lungs healthy. (2003, June). *Environmental Nutrition, 26*(6), 1, 6. Retrieved from http://www .environmentalnutrition.com

- Always give inclusive page numbers for an article, even if you are viewing it in an HTML environment that is unpaginated; for this reason, if you have a choice it may be better to view the article in PDF, where the original pagination is preserved. If you have found the article through an online database, usually the database citation will provide the page numbers.

6. How do I cite a film or television broadcast?

- For a film, the producer's names go in the "author" position, followed by the directors' names. Give the name of the country where the film was produced, as well as the production company.

Bartlett, S., LeRose, M., & Ridout, S. (Producers), & Bartlett, S. & Le Rose, M. (Directors). (2008). *Desperately seeking doctors* [Motion picture]. Canada: Dreamfilm Productions & Canadian Broadcasting Corporation.

continued

- For a television broadcast, follow the format for a chapter in a book, treating the individual episode as the "chapter" and the series as the "book." Treat the writer(s) and director(s) as the "authors," and the producer(s) or executive producer(s) as the "editor."

Kelley, M., MacIntyre, L., & McKeown, B. (Writers), Docherty, N., Houlihan, R., Karp, M., Rumak, O. J., Vickery, C., Weinstein, T., & Elash, A. (Producers/Directors). (2013, April 12). Rate my hospital [Television series episode]. In J. Williamson (Executive producer), *The fifth estate*. Toronto, Canada: CBC.

BOX 4.3 | **Sample List of References**

References

Adinoff, A. (2002, August). Quality of care and outcomes of adults with asthma treated by specialists and generalists in managed care. *Pediatrics, 110*(2), 454. Retrieved from http://pediatrics.aappublications.org

Barnes, P. J. (2003). New concepts in chronic obstructive pulmonary disease. *Annual Review of Medicine, 54*, 113–130. doi:10.1146/annurev.med.54.101601.152209

Grimes, G. C., Manning, J. L., Patel, P., Via, M. R. (2007). Medication for COPD: A review of effectiveness. *American Family Physician, 76*(8), 1141–1147.

Lee, T. A., Weaver, F. M., & Weiss, K. B. (2007, January). Impact of pneumococcal vaccination on pneumonia rates in patients with COPD and asthma. *JGIM: Journal of General Internal Medicine, 22*(1), 62–67. doi: 10.1007/s11606-007-0118-3

Moore, W. C. (2009, May 15). Update in asthma 2008. *American Journal of Respiratory and Critical Care Medicine, 179*(10), 869–875. doi:10.1164/rccm.200902-0290UP

Public Health Agency of Canada. (2006, May). Asthma. *It's your health*. Retrieved from http://www.hc-sc.gc.ca/hl-vs/iyh-vsv/diseases-maladies/asthm-eng.php

Stockley, R. A., Rennard, S., Rabe, K., & Celli, B. (2007). *Chronic obstructive pulmonary disease*. New Jersey: Wiley-Blackwell.

TRY IT YOURSELF

1. Prepare a list of at least five references in APA style for the sources found in the researching exercise on p. 106.

2. Take five books off your bookshelf and prepare a list of references for them.

Why do you think it is important to follow APA format when preparing an essay or report?

CHAPTER LINKS FOR FURTHER EXPLORATION

- **OWL at Purdue (http://owl.english.purdue.edu/owl/section/2/10)**

Purdue University's Online Writing Lab is a valuable resource for APA style, as well as other writing-related information.

- **APA Style (http://www.apastyle.org)**

The APA's official website provides information about APA style and includes tutorials and quick answers to commonly asked questions. It also contains a link to the APA Style Blog.

- **Haig, J., MacMillan, V., & Raikes, G. (2014).** *Cites & sources: An APA documentation guide* (4th ed.). Toronto: Nelson.

Your college or university may have a reference tool such as RefWorks that allows you to create your list of references easily as you research. Visit your library or refer to its website for more information. (Be aware, however, that even if your list of References is created by a software tool such as RefWorks, you are responsible for double-checking all details for accuracy of information and formatting.)

5

WRITING IN A PROFESSIONAL SETTING

At the end of this chapter, you should be able to

- produce effective resumés and cover letters
- review sample resumés and cover letters to determine their strengths and weaknesses
- write professional letters and emails in the allied health workplace
- determine the advantages and disadvantages of both the direct and the indirect letter/email
- understand how to write narrative progress notes and structured progress notes (e.g., SOAP, DAR, PIE)
- determine the advantages and disadvantages of both the structured and the unstructured progress note
- recognize the influence of technology in medical documentation and record-keeping

INTRODUCTION

Previous chapters prepared you to meet the writing demands of your college or university health sciences program. Now it is time to prepare you for what you have strived so hard for: being successful in the health care workplace.

Graduation from college or university followed by entrance into the workplace is an exciting time in most people's lives. After the financial and time investments of a postsecondary education, it is time to reap the rewards of the educational investment that you have made. There is nothing worse than putting effort and discipline into a college or university degree only to face challenges securing a job after graduation.

To reduce the chances of this occurring, the first step in successfully transitioning from school to workplace is the creation of an effective resumé and cover letter that will demonstrate to potential employers why you are the best candidate for the health care job that interests you. This is exactly what you will learn to do at the outset of this chapter.

Then, once you have landed your desired health care job (because of your top-notch resumé), you will need to demonstrate on a daily basis that you can meet the writing demands of your particular profession. The section on professional correspondence in this chapter guides you toward this goal by providing some useful tips on presenting yourself professionally and diplomatically in your everyday written communication.

Finally, this chapter concludes by introducing you to the most common ways that health care professionals like nurses, paramedics, occupational therapists, and physio-therapists document and monitor patient health. To this end, the final section of this chapter provides a basic overview of the progress note, structured and unstructured, as well as the advantages and disadvantages of computerized documentation systems.

RESUMÉS AND COVER LETTERS

While you will write many important documents in your professional life, the cover letter and resumé are the two documents that will open professional doors for you. Many people underestimate the importance of these documents. Your cover letter and resumé inform prospective employers about more than just your education and experience: they demonstrate your attention to detail and ability to communicate clearly—crucial skills in the allied health professions.

> *I was hiring a pharmacy assistant and I received many resumés from qualified applicants. One recent college graduate had the required education and experience; however, he misspelled several words—including "pharmacy" and the name of his college—on his resumé. In my business, one tiny mistake can have tragic consequences; we can't afford to hire someone who is careless. This applicant did not get the job.*
>
> —Pharmacist, Winnipeg, MB

The Goals of Your Resumé and Cover Letter

1. Grab the reader's attention.

   DO ... use catchy headings that are relevant to the position you are applying for.
   DO ... use a professional and consistent layout.
   DO ... make it visually appealing.
   DON'T ... use coloured paper or ink.

2. Capture the reader's interest.

> DO … clearly identify your key traits.
> DO … highlight skills and experiences that are relevant for the position.
> DO … show why you would be an asset to the organization.
> DON'T … lie, or even exaggerate.

3. Encourage the reader to contact you.

> DO … offer to provide more information, such as work samples and ideas.
> DO … ask for an interview.
> DO … provide your phone number and email address.
> DON'T … provide unprofessional email addresses—sexyvixen@hotmail.com does not fit the image of a competent health care professional!

The Resume

Your resumé provides your prospective employer with a summary of your skills, qualities, and experience. Frequently, employers receive more than one hundred applications for a single position; therefore, they may look at each resumé for less than a minute. How can you make a positive impression and become one of the very few selected for an interview?

Tips for Writing Your Resumé

1. Use titles or headings that match the jobs you want.

   - If applying for a nursing position, you may choose to use the heading "Nursing Qualifications."

2. Create a design that attracts attention and identifies your key attributes.

   - Most resumés include the following sections: Skills/Qualifications; Employment Experience; Education. You may also want to add Academic Accomplishments or Personal Attributes, depending on your strongest qualities. Ask yourself what sets you apart from other applicants. Put that information first.

3. Customize your resume to every job.

   - Emphasize the skills and experience that are suited to the particular job you are applying for. List skills in order of relevance.

4. Use key words from the job advertisement.

   - Employers carefully select the wording of an advertisement to reflect the qualities that they see as important. Read the ad carefully, and use the same key words (for example, "collaborate with…," "assess extent of…," "document and record…").

5. Use "accomplishment words" (see Box 5.1).

- These words indicate that you have made significant contributions to your previous workplaces or educational institutions.

BOX 5.1	Accomplishment Words	
achieved	improved	remodelled
activated	increased	reorganized
addressed	initiated	represented
administered	launched	researched
built	led	restructured
conducted	motivated	shaped
consulted	operated	solved
created	organized	stimulated
demonstrated	overhauled	strengthened
developed	performed	supervised
enabled	planned	trained
engineered	prepared	upgraded
facilitated	presented	worked
guided	produced	wrote
identified	recommended	
implemented	reduced	

Matthew Lui

3607-19th St. SE
Calgary, AB
T5A 0B4
(403) 555-5555
Email: mattlui@hotmail.com

EDUCATION

Pharmacy Technician Diploma   April 2008

Bow Valley College, Calgary, AB

WORK EXPERIENCE

Work Experience section uses accomplishment words (*checked, assisted, maintained, consulted, provided, handled, and referred*) to highlight the applicant's positive impact on past places of employment.

Pharmacy Assistant (Co-op)   Jan 2006–April 2007

- Checked invoices to ensure accuracy of client information
- Assisted pharmacist with dispensing prescriptions
- Maintained inventory, checked expired drugs

Cashier   Jan 2003–Dec 2003

Millerdale Pharmacy, Red Deer, AB

- Consulted with customers to determine their needs and provide suggestions
- Provided excellent customer service and product knowledge
- Handled and referred customer inquiries

Source: Adapted from documents provided by Humber College's Career Services

Anna Petersen

60 Clipper Road, #706
Toronto, ON M2J 4E2
(416) 497-3294
Email: apetersen@hotmail.com

PERSONAL PROFILE

- Communicates and interacts effectively with individuals on all levels
- Brings enthusiasm and devotion to encourage a client-oriented environment
- Assists staff, clients, and supervisors in identifying and resolving problems
- Works well with others toward achieving team goals or alone as an individual

RELEVANT PROFESSIONAL EXPERIENCE

Emergency Services—Registered Nurse	Toronto, ON
Closing the Gap Healthcare Group	March 2008–Present
Emergency Services—Registered Nurse	Toronto, ON
SRT MED-STAFF	December 2006–March 2008
Emergency Services—Registered Nurse	Toronto, ON
St. Joseph's Health Centre	January 2006–December 2006

EDUCATION

Bachelor of Science with Honours—Nursing	2000–2005
York University/Seneca College	
Social Service Worker—Gerontology	1999–2000
Seneca College of Applied Arts & Technology	
Emergency First Aid—Level C and CPR Certified	

VOLUNTEER EXPERIENCE

Private Tutor	2000–2009
Multiple Sclerosis Society	2005–2008
Heart & Stroke Foundation	2005–2008

> Volunteer experience gives the impression that the applicant is caring and compassionate, and values experience over money.

The Curriculum Vitae

Later in your career, you may prepare a curriculum vitae (CV) instead of a resumé. While a resume is brief and concise (usually one or two pages), a CV is a longer, more detailed summary of your educational background, publications, presentations, research and/or teaching experience, awards, and professional affiliations. A CV should be used when applying for teaching or research positions, or when applying for fellowships or grants.

The Cover Letter

Never discount the importance of the cover letter—it is the basis for your reader's first impression of you. A cover letter shouldn't just summarize your resume; it should draw the reader's attention to your strengths, highlighting those qualities that set you apart from the competition.

The Parts of a Cover Letter

1. Introduction

   - Tell the reader what position you are applying for and where you saw the advertisement.
   - Briefly explain why you want to work for this organization and why you want this specific position.

2. Body

   - Briefly outline your best qualities and your most relevant skills for the job.
   - State how your skills would benefit the company.

3. Conclusion

   - Clearly ask for an interview. Provide contact information.

Tips for Writing Your Cover Letter

1. Include your data and the recipient's data at the top of the page.

   - Include your name, address, phone number(s), email address.
   - Include the recipient's work title, address, and name (if available). If you do not know the recipient's name, use the title given in the advertisement. "Dear Human Resources" or "Dear Hiring Manager" is preferable to "To Whom It May Concern."

2. Keep it simple and direct.

- Employers often receive hundreds of applications for one job opening; you have about 30 seconds to get your message across.
- A cover letter should fit on one page.

3. Do not omit necessary information.

- Include all information specifically requested, such as availability and salary expectations.

4. Proofread carefully and read out loud to check style and flow.

- A single error can cause the reader to reject your application.

5. Make your letter a reflection of you.

- Customize your letter to fit each position.
- Avoid clichés ("I'm a people person").
- Do not make any claims that you cannot back up with actions.

One of the core values of our health care organization is to "treat everyone with respect and dignity." As you know, Toronto is a multicultural city, and staff must work with colleagues and patients of different ethnicities. It is important that candidates understand and respect diversity. I've seen some candidates write standard blanket statements that they "work well with and get along with other people." In one interview, one of the questions I asked was, "What type of people do you not like to work with?" The candidate looked carefully around the room to make sure no one was around, and very quietly said to me, "Well, to be honest with you, I don't like to work too much with black people." Needless to say, I was in shock, and this closed the door to any job opportunities for this person. Moral of the story: Understand the mission, vision, and values of the organization to which you are applying. Ensure that your cover letter and resumé truly and accurately reflect who you are and align with the culture of that organization. Don't say things you don't mean, as the truth will likely come out in the interview when you least expect it.

—Supervisor, University Health Network, Toronto

Jasmeet Singh

76-3468 Drummond Street
Montreal, Quebec
H3G 1Y4
514-842-5293
singhj@gmail.com

June 20, 2013
273 Pine Lane
Montreal, Quebec
L5L 2X8

Dear Jason Bote,

It is with great interest and enthusiasm that I am applying for the position of Case Manager, which was advertised in the *Globe and Mail* on Wednesday, June 19, 2013. I am tremendously excited at the prospect of working in a facility that is known for its excellence in all aspects of patient care. I strongly believe that my three years of nursing experience will allow me to create an immediate and positive impact within your excellent facility.

Throughout my clinical placement, I have successfully increased productivity and efficiency, and have clearly demonstrated my ability to manage multiple projects and tasks concurrently with excellent follow-through and attention to quality.

I have illustrated exceptional communication and leadership skills through my work with individuals at all levels, and have been highly effective in establishing rapport with clients, co-workers, and management.

You will benefit from my ability to foster a desired sense of comfort and deliver superior client-centred care. I have consistently displayed strong interpersonal skills and a genuine interest in meeting the needs of individuals, families, and the community at large.

I am enthusiastic and eager about working in a role that is ideally suited to my personal qualities and professional skills. An interview will provide us with an opportunity to discuss our needs and demonstrate further how I can add great value to your organization. You may reach me at 514-842-5293. I look forward to hearing from you, and thank you for your consideration.

Sincerely,

Jasmeet Singh

The letter opens by demonstrating the applicant's enthusiasm, identifying which position is being applied for and where it was advertised, and highlighting the qualities and experiences that make the applicant well-suited for the job.

This shows the impact that the applicant has had on his former place of work and implies that he can make the same improvements in his next job.

This shows that he communicates well with others and is a team player. Note the use of the word "effective."

Here, the applicant clearly outlines the benefits for the entire organization.

The applicant closes by reiterating his enthusiasm, telling the reader why he wants the position, and showing why he is right for the position. He then requests an interview, suggesting that he wants the opportunity to prove that he is the right person for the job.

1. Find an advertisement for a job in your chosen field and tailor your resumé for it, using the suggestions from this chapter. Write a cover letter to accompany it. Don't forget to proofread both very carefully. Exchange with a classmate and critique each other's letter and resumé as if you were an employer.

PROFESSIONAL CORRESPONDENCE

Until the last decade, there were two main forms of professional correspondence: memos, which were used to communicate within an organization, and letters, which were used to communicate outside an organization. Recently, however, electronic correspondence has replaced both documents. There are many benefits to email: it reduces response time, it saves paper, and it provides an electronic record of your correspondence.

However, many people fail to distinguish between casual and professional emails, which can lead to misunderstandings and loss of credibility. There are several things to keep in mind when writing emails in an academic or professional setting.

Tips for Writing Professional Emails

1. Provide a clear and specific subject heading.

    - This prevents emails from being rejected as spam and allows the recipient to prioritize his or her messages.
    - Example: Revised August Schedule for Floor 3 Nurses.

2. Begin your email with a proper greeting, just as you would in a written letter.

    - This shows respect for the recipient and establishes a formal tone.
    - Example: Dear Dr. Singh; Dear Kevin; Dear Professor Sinopoli.
    - Be sure to check the spelling of names.

3. Identify yourself.

    - Always sign your name.
    - When writing to a teacher, include your full name and course/section number.
    - When writing to a professional colleague, include your job title and department or division.

4. Follow the standards of academic or professional writing.

    - Write in complete, grammatically correct sentences.
    - Use a professional font (e.g., Times Roman, Arial), size, and colour.
    - Use standard spelling, punctuation, and capitalization.

5. Keep the email brief.

- The message should fit on one screen.
- Each email should be limited to one subject. Do not confuse your reader by attempting to deal with multiple issues in one email.

6. Pause before sending.

- Check for spelling, punctuation, and grammar errors.
- Ask yourself if the content of your email is appropriate. If your boss were to see it, what would his or her reaction be?

7. Use a serious, professional tone.

- Jokes and sarcasm may be misinterpreted as rude and/or insulting.

Before composing your email, ask yourself two questions: 1) Who is your audience? 2) What is the purpose of your email? The answers to these questions will determine the content, tone, and structure of your email.

Direct vs. Indirect Structure

There are two basic structures for business correspondence—direct and indirect.

Direct

If your reader is going to be pleased or neutral about your message, and if the information is fairly straightforward, then you can use the direct structure. In a direct email, you begin with the main point and follow it up with any necessary details or explanations. Most business correspondence follows the direct pattern; it saves the reader time by getting right to the point.

Indirect

There are some situations in which your reader will be resistant to or displeased with your message, such as when you are delivering bad news or denying a request. In these situations, the indirect structure will help minimize the negative reaction, by giving the explanation and context before delivering the bad news. This approach shows respect for the reader's feelings, and encourages the reader to try to understand the entire situation rather than react instinctively to the main point.

BOX 5.2 **Direct and Indirect Emails**

Dear Mr. Santiago,

We are pleased to inform you that your proposal has been accepted for presentation at the 2014 CCHC National Conference.

Please register on the conference website www.cchc.conference.ca, where you will also find travel and hotel information.

Thank you for sharing your work with us, and we look forward to seeing you at the conference.

Best,

David Brulé, PhD

CCHC Conference Chair

Dear Mr. Santiago,

Thank you for your recent proposal submission for the 2014 CCHC National Conference. This year we received a record number of submissions, and the large volume of interesting proposals made the selection process particularly difficult. Each proposal was reviewed by several experts in the field, and unfortunately, your proposal was not selected for inclusion.

Thank you once again for submitting your work, and we hope to see you at the conference.

Best,

David Brulé, PhD

CCHC Conference Chair

Raising or Responding to Sensitive Issues in an Email

While face-to-face communication is ideal for discussing sensitive issues (requests, complaints, conflicts, and so on), sometimes an email is necessary to either request a meeting, follow up on an earlier conversation, or respond to a situation. In such cases, follow these guidelines:

1. Briefly state the history and context of the issue.

2. Outline any actions you have taken to resolve the issue.

3. Give reasons that it is necessary for this issue to be resolved quickly.

4. Suggest possible solutions.

5. If the issue is particularly complicated or sensitive, or if nothing is resolved after a few emails, request a face-to-face meeting.

6. Keep your tone neutral. Avoid sounding aggressive, threatening, or defensive.

7. If you are emotional about the issue, compose the email and then wait a day before sending. Re-read your message carefully to avoid saying anything you could regret later. Consider showing it to a friend or family member for feedback.

8. Check grammar, spelling, and punctuation carefully.

Think about the last time you received bad news in an email. Did the author use the indirect structure? What was your reaction to the email? Could the news have been delivered more effectively?

Now think about a time when you delivered bad news in an email. How did you structure the message? How was the message received? Would you do anything differently if you were writing the email today?

The subject line clearly identifies the sender. This is especially important if your email address does not contain your full name. Avoid a subject line such as "Request," as one professor could receive over 100 such messages before a major assignment or exam.

To: lawrence_chan@brandonu.ca
From: dylan_cornacchia@brandonu.ca

Subject: Dylan Cornacchia, Student # 9945023

The email opens with a greeting, and refers to the recipient by name.

Dear Professor Chan,

I am a student in your section of Nursing Foundations II that meets Tuesdays and Thursdays.

The writer clearly explains the problem in full sentences.

The course outline indicates that we have a test scheduled for Tuesday, March 10. I have a medical condition that requires frequent specialists' appointments, and there is an appointment scheduled for the same time as the test. I tried to reschedule the appointment, but there is a three-month waiting period.

The writer offers documentation, showing that the problem is a legitimate one.

My doctor's office is sending me a note showing that I do have an appointment at that time. I will give it to you when I receive it.

The next step is to suggest a solution to the problem, inquiring whether this is an acceptable solution for the recipient of the email.

Is it possible for me to write the test on an earlier or later date? Please let me know what I can do to avoid losing the marks for this test. If you would like to discuss this issue in person, I can meet you during your office hours next week.

Best,

Dylan Cornacchia

To: David Bernstein <david_bernstein@ssc.ca
From: Florence Nguyen <Florence_nguyen@ssc.ca>

Subject: Violet Abela

Dear Mr. Bernstein,

From our brief conversation this morning, I understand that you received a phone call from Mrs. Symington, expressing her dissatisfaction with the treatment her mother (Ms. Violet Abela) is receiving.

I have been working with Ms. Abela for three weeks now, and I am confident that I have followed protocol and behaved professionally. In addition, I have noticed a marked improvement in Ms. Abela's range of motion.

I understand that Mrs. Symington has raised similar complaints over the three months her mother has been a resident here. The satisfaction of our clients and their families is very important to me. I would be happy if we could meet soon to discuss this further.

Regards,

Florence Nguyen
OTA
Sunnyside Seniors' Centre

The writer begins with a formal salutation, as in a letter. If you are on friendly terms with the recipient, use his or her first name, but be professional.

The context of the situation is clearly stated. If your email is in response to an earlier conversation or correspondence, indicate this.

The writer provides her opinion of the situation in a clear, non-defensive manner.

The writer gives more context and emphasizes her desire to reach a solution. She ends with a request for a face-to-face meeting.

The letter concludes respectfully ("regards") and includes the writer's full name and position.

TRY IT YOURSELF

1. Rewrite the following email, to make it more appropriate and effective.

To: brian.simpson@senecac.on.ca

From: prettygirl@hotmail.com

Subject: Just a reminder

Hey Sir, I was wondering if it were possible to boost my final mark by 3%. I'm sort 3% to receive the scholarship of $1000. At this point i will have to go to summer school just to get 3%. PLEASE PLEASE PLEASE PLEASE i tried me hardest. If you can, it would mean a lot to me and will also assist in my finical situation. I will take anything you can give if possible. Thanks! Amanpreet ☺

2. You have been working as a health care professional in a probationary capacity for six months. This is your first job in the field. While your six-month performance evaluation says you are enthusiastic and devoted, it also states that you are, on occasion, insufficiently focused on your job and sometimes seem to be lost. Furthermore, you have been late to work twice in the past three months. Finally, your supervisor says you sometimes lack patience.

While flawless performance evaluations are not expected—especially after only six months—you know that this could affect your chances of being hired back at the end of the year.

Write an email to your boss, offering your interpretation of the evaluation and trying to convince him or her that you are indeed a capable employee. Make up any necessary details, including names and dates.

CHARACTERISTICS OF GOOD PROFESSIONAL WRITING

Communicate your message in CLEAR language. Professional writing should be direct and to the point; if the reader doesn't know what you are trying to say, he or she will probably not bother reading further. If you are asking that action be taken, be sure to state precisely what the desired outcome is.

When providing information about an incident or issue, be sure to remain OBJECTIVE. Do not resort to accusations or name-calling. State the facts, and leave the emotions out.

Health care professionals are busy; therefore, professional correspondence should be CONCISE. Keep emails to one screen-length. Keep resumés and letters to one page.

Present your information in an ORGANIZED manner. In letters and emails, begin with a greeting, followed by your reason for writing, a summary of the issue, a proposed solution, and a call for action.

Check your facts to ensure that you are presenting an ACCURATE picture of the situation. Facts can be checked, so never stretch the truth in a resumé, letter, or email.

Always proofread professional correspondence to ensure that it is grammatically CORRECT. Errors can reduce your credibility in the eyes of your employer, colleagues, or professor.

Adopt an AUDIENCE-APPROPRIATE tone. Avoid abbreviations (lol) and emoticons (☺).

Provide a THOROUGH picture of whatever you are presenting, whether it be a patient's history, an on-the-job conflict, or your own employment history. Include all necessary information, including dates, quantities, and the like. If information is too sensitive to include in an email, request an appointment to speak in person.

DOCUMENTATION SYSTEMS IN HEALTH CARE FACILITIES

Now that you have secured that desired health care job through the creation of a proper cover letter and resumé, it is time to look at the specific types of writing you will be doing once you start working with patients.

© vgstudio / Shutterstock

The Progress Note

There are many different ways of documenting a patient's condition throughout the caregiving process, and the type of documentation required will depend on your health care role, as well as on the requirements of the facility where you work. One of the most important documents in the health care workplace is the progress note. A **progress note** is a document that records, tracks, and monitors a patient's health status. While formats and styles of progress notes vary, health care professionals like doctors, nurses, psychiatrists, and personal support workers are all responsible for carefully documenting observations and assessments of their patients from the point of admission through to the point of discharge. In acute care facilities, health care workers are required to frequently update a patient's health status. So, with all the writing that is required in a health care institution, it is a good idea to get into good writing habits now. Below, you will be introduced to two common types of progress notes: the narrative note and the structured note (e.g., SOAP, SOAPIE, SOAPIER, DAR, PIE).

The Narrative Note

Traditionally, narrative notes that read like mini-stories were the main way that health care providers documented patient care. Today, while most health care facilities seem to prefer more structured patient notes, some institutions still require that a patient's health be updated using the narrative note.

Advantages

- Narrative charting is easy to learn. There are no complicated formulas or formatting procedures to remember.
- Because narrative charting does not require a lot in terms of format and style, it is flexible and adaptable to various facilities.
- Narrative charting can be an effective way to convey health intentions and patient responses.
- The narrative format can help personalize the patient–caregiver relationship as the patient's health is not reduced to an acronym or formula.

Disadvantages

- A lack of formatting requirements can lead to inconsistency in record-keeping, which may sacrifice quality of patient care.
- As a mini-story, this type of progress note can appear less scientific than some of the more structured formats like SOAP, PIE, and DAR and may encourage the incorporation of too much subjective detail.
- The narrative style can lead to "over-charting," particularly for new workers who need time to master how to distinguish essential detail from non-essential detail.
- Because of its lack of a fixed organizational structure, repetition of detail can result.
- It can be difficult for readers of the unstructured narrative note to find specific information quickly and effortlessly.

As you can see in the sample narrative note below, relevant patient information is presented as a mini-story.

Sample narrative note

June 26, 2009 @ 0745:
Pt. was aware and alert this morning and oriented to time, place, and person. Pt. observably distressed, tearful, and anxious. While discussing pt's needs, pt. expressed anxiety and fear with regard to his current health experience. Stated, "I am so afraid of dying," and "It's my family that seems unable to let me go and say goodbye." Discussed with pt. his fears of dying and proposed grief-counselling services; also offered to call a family member for added support. Pt. observably less anxious and distressed post-interview. Informs that current plan of care and proposed services are satisfactory to his needs and that he does not wish to see any relatives at present. VS otherwise consistent; BP 120/60, HR 65 regular, O2 98% RA, RR 18, T-36.9 tympanic. Skin pink, warm, and dry. Chest clear, abdomen soft, no tenderness. IV in situ and infusing well NS at 100cc/hr. At present no acute concerns. Will follow through with proposed plan of care and monitor ongoing. Call bell within reach. Winter Eve Hill RN

Source: Courtesy of Winter Eve Hill.

The Structured Note (SOAP, SOAPIE, and SOAPIER)

Structured progress notes can be organized in many different ways, as you will see. Despite differences in formatting and organization of the structured progress note, the categories of focus are similar and include variations on the following themes: problem, assessment, intervention, and evaluation. Workplaces have different preferences when it comes to charting formalities, so it is best to check with your workplace to see what method of documentation they prefer.

Advantages

- Acronyms like SOAP, PIE, and DAR are easy to remember and are effective ways of setting up and organizing patient information.
- As caregivers rely on the same structure to create their notes, there is consistency in the documentation process.
- Consistent and organized recording of relevant information can result in better communication and decreased levels of frustration.
- Other team members can easily locate useful and relevant patient data because of the clearly defined and consistently ordered categories of information.

Disadvantages

- There are concerns that the formulaic nature of structured progress notes does not allow for a comprehensive account of the patient's progress.
- Sometimes additional or supplementary notes may be required for important information that does not fit into any of the SOAP, DAR, or PIE formulas.
- Training is required for health care professionals to properly understand and correctly use structured progress notes.

The SOAP note

S = subjective

Subjective detail includes what the patient and his or her caregivers tell you about the symptoms that are of concern. Recording a patient's exact words is preferred to paraphrasing.

O = objective

Objective data includes the health care provider's observation of the patient (body language, affect) and records vital signs, test results, and medications given.

A = assessment

The assessment of the patient's condition is based on an evaluation of both subjective and objective data.

P = plan

Based on the assessment, a treatment plan is documented. The treatment plan should include both long-term and short-term measures.

Sometimes facilities require an extension of the SOAP format. You may be asked to use SOAPIE or SOAPIER.

I = intervention

This section can be used to record a change in treatment plan.

E = evaluation

Here, the treatment plan is evaluated for progress and effect.

R = revision

Based on the outcome and evaluation of the treatment plan, revisions or recommendations might be necessary and are recorded here.

Sample SOAP note

June 26, 2009 @ 0745:

S: "I am so afraid of dying. How will my family support themselves; how will I cope with the pain? I can't believe this is happening to me, and yet, strangely, I'm ready. It's my family that seems unable to let me go and say goodbye."

O: Pt. presents with observable anxiety and distress related to his current health experience. Pt. expresses his fears of death, and the pain that may be related to it, as well as his family's inability to let him go and accept that his life may be nearing the end.

A: Pt. afraid of death and dying and has anxiety related to his family's future, as well as their inability to accept the possibility of his passing.

P: Grief counsellor called to bedside to assist and support both the pt. and his family during his current health experience. Care plan regarding pain management and pt's present needs discussed briefly with pt. Winter Eve Hill RN

Source: Courtesy of Winter Eve Hill.

The PIE note

P = problem

> This is similar to the subjective detail recorded in the SOAP note. The problem is the patient's reason for seeking help or assistance.

I = intervention

> This is a record of how the patient's health concern was addressed. This might include the prescription of medication or a referral to a health specialist.

E = evaluation

> Here the health care worker provides an evaluation of the effectiveness of the proposed intervention strategies.

Sample PIE Note

> June 26, 2009 @ 1005:
>
> **P:** Called to bedside. Pt. received in observable distress. C/o severe RLQ abdo pain, 8/10. Grimacing and writhing in bed, clutching abdomen.
>
> **I:** 6mg Morphine with 50cc NS given via IV. Pt. repositioned in bed.
>
> **E:** Pt. states pain has decreased to 3/10, 15 mins post analgesia. Resting comfortably at present. Denies any further needs. Will monitor ongoing for therapeutic effect of pain management and administer analgesia as required. Winter Eve Hill RN

Source: Courtesy of Winter Eve Hill.

The DAR note

D = data

In the DAR note, all subjective and objective data is recorded in the same section.

A = action

This is an account of the proposed care plan based on the assembled health data.

R = response

The patient's responses to the implemented interventions are recorded here.

Sample DAR note

> June 26, 2009 @ 0745:
>
> **D:** Pt. received observably distressed. Expressed anxiety and fear with regard to his current health experience. Fearful of death and dying, and concerned that he may experience pain. Pt. expressed his anxiety and distress related to his family's future, and is concerned that they have not yet accepted his current health status and the possibility of his passing.
>
> **A:** Discussed with pt. his current plan of care, and discussed his potential needs for pain management and therapy. Called grief counsellor to bedside for both pt. and family support.
>
> **R:** Pt. expressed a great deal of relief with regard to his current plan of care and pain management, as well as proposed services. Observably more comfortable and less anxious. Pt. denies any further needs at present; will evaluate therapeutic effect of pain management as well as supportive services ongoing throughout the day. Winter Eve Hill RN

Source: Courtesy of Winter Eve Hill.

CHARTING BY EXCEPTION

In the high stress and fast pace of the busy health care environment, the "no frills" approach to patient charting, known as charting by exception (CBE), is becoming an increasingly popular way to document patient progress. CBE requires that only significant or abnormal health occurrences are recorded, thereby eliminating lengthy and repetitive notes. In this type of charting, the caregiver uses tick charts or flow sheets to record abnormal activity.

Advantages

- The time spent on the task of documenting a patient's health progress is significantly decreased by recording only abnormal activity.
- Tick and flow sheets eliminate the need for lengthy and time-consuming notes.
- Changes and concerns in a patient's health are easily spotted.
- CBE is usually done at the patient's bedside, allowing the immediate recording of data, which may decrease documentation errors that result from delayed charting or charting after the fact.

Disadvantages

- There is a concern that a comprehensive account of a patient's condition cannot be achieved by focusing only on the problematic.
- CBE requires an extensive repository of flow sheets customized to reflect the variety of medical experiences that health care workers encounter in a care facility.
- CBE appears to focus on obvious changes, potentially neglecting less obvious but nonetheless important changes.
- Sometimes CBE notes need to be supplemented with progress notes, which detract from the goal of efficiency.
- The development of guidelines and standards of care required to use CBE is time-consuming.
- The caregiver has to demonstrate knowledge of established assessment guidelines in order to use CBE properly.
- Caregivers have to receive training and practice in CBE.

DOCUMENTATION AND THE COMPUTER

© Ioana Drutu / Shutterstock

Practically all health care facilities today rely to some extent on computerized documentation systems. Computerized medical information systems allow the health care worker to access a wide range of important patient data by simply entering a personal access code or password.

Advantages

- Efficiency of documentation is increased, particularly if computers are placed at patients' bedsides for immediate recording of data.
- Basic computer fonts are much easier to read than handwritten notes.
- With electronic storage of information, medical data can be centralized.
- Clinical and statistical data can easily be calculated and retrieved.
- Computers have the capability of reducing some documentation errors as many current systems provide an alert message if patient data is entered incorrectly or not at all.

Disadvantages

- Medical records are private matters and computer systems raise questions about the confidentiality and security of such data.
- The assumption exists that health care workers will have the essential computer skills to succeed in an electronic environment.
- If technology used in a medical facility breaks down, this may cause significant lapses in care as well as loss of valuable data, which could potentially be life-threatening.
- Electronic systems can be expensive to install and maintain.
- Standardized forms and databases raise the concern of whether individualization of patient care is compromised.

- Computerized documentation depends on the accuracy of information entered by the health care worker.
- The computer can aid in efficiency but does not provide the personal contact and connection that are central to the patient–caregiver relationship.

MEDICAL FORMS

Aside from potential charting duties, as a future health care provider you will be required to fill out numerous other forms based on your professional role and the requirements of the facility where you work. Whether your facility requires you to fill out forms electronically or by hand, when filling out medical forms in the workplace make sure you abide by the following rules:

- Be neat and legible on handwritten forms.
- Date and sign everything. Additionally, be sure to include your credentials along with your signature.
- Follow the procedure dictated by your workplace for correcting errors, both handwritten and electronic.
- Educate yourself on the documentation codes and abbreviations used in your particular workplace.
- Make sure you are competent in basic computer functions like keyboarding and that you are able to successfully navigate the electronic information management system used by your health care facility.
- Maintain your password's confidentiality at all times.
- When using computerized health information systems, always remember to log off when you are no longer using the system.

CHAPTER LINKS FOR FURTHER EXPLORATION

- **Health Care Job Search (http://www.healthcarejob.ca)**

This site provides access to healthcare jobs across Canada.

- **OSCAR Canada (http://www.oscarcanada.org)**

OSCAR is an open-source Electronic Medical Records (EMR) software program used by front-line health care professionals. The site includes screenshots, demos, and useful templates for electronic progress notes.

- **College of Registered Nurses of Nova Scotia. (2012). *Documentation Guidelines for Registered Nurses*. Halifax: College of Registered Nurses of Nova Scotia. Retrieved from http://www.crnns.ca/documents/DocumentationGuidelines.pdf**

This helpful document provides guidelines for professional accountability in documentation and describes the expectations for nursing documentation, including electronic documentation.

ETHICS AND DOCUMENTATION

At the end of this chapter, you should be able to

- understand the importance of ethics in the health care workplace use and apply ethics-related terminology including *morality, ethics, ethical inquiry, ethical principle, ethical challenge,* and *ethical dilemma*
- discuss eight ethical principles in health care and note their relevance to important documents like the Code of Ethics, advanced directive form, and express consent form
- determine appropriate courses of action in ethically challenging health care scenarios

INTRODUCTION

Although the field of ethics is laden with questions and short on conclusive answers, one thing is certain: any time we are dealing with human life, ethical discussion and debate become essential. While health care workers have always dealt with human lives and the complexity of issues that arise as a result, rapid technological developments blur the boundaries of what it means to be human more than ever before and make for some increasingly complex health decisions. In this chapter, you will see that ethical challenges, while part of the job for the health care professional, are certainly not an easy part of that job. As you have learned in previous chapters, patient well-being should be the ultimate focus of the health care provider; the achievement of quality patient care can be difficult, however, when other factors compete with and challenge such quality.

In this chapter, you will be introduced to terminology that will provide you with the requisite vocabulary to engage in important discussions on the topic of ethics and health. In addition, you will receive an introduction to eight ethical principles commonly used by health care providers to determine appropriate response and behaviour in ethically challenging situations. As well, you will discover the close relationship between ethics and documentation, and see how crucial documents in the health care workplace like the Code of Ethics and consent and advanced directive forms are constructed with ethical query in mind. Finally, you will have the opportunity to apply the various aspects of ethics presented to challenging, but realistic, health care scenarios.

IMPORTANT DEFINITIONS

While *morality* refers to what people believe to be right or wrong, the term *ethics* refers to the analysis and reflection of why we believe something is right or wrong. Consequently, *ethical inquiry* is the process we go through when trying to determine our responses and actions to dilemmas that pose no obvious or easy solutions. An *ethical dilemma* can be defined as a situation where there is conflict between competing *ethical principles*: rules that guide our moral conduct and provide a foundation for ethical decision-making. Finally, an *ethical challenge* refers to situations where there is a conflict between knowledge and will: situations where one knows the right thing to do but for a variety of reasons, which commonly include fear and/or negative repercussions, is reluctant to act ethically. Ethics, in making us accountable for our moral convictions and our behaviours, allows us to engage in important discussions concerning personal responsibility, professional responsibility, community responsibility, and universal responsibility. Ethics also requires that we consider many important questions when confronted with challenging choices: What is the best course of action in a given situation? Why is this the best course of action? How have I arrived at my decision? What is my decision based on? What should my decision be based on?

ETHICS IN THE HEALTH SCIENCES

In the course of any given day, most workplaces are confronted with ethical challenges or dilemmas and, in the health care workplace, where practitioners deal with matters of mortality and quality of life daily, such scenarios are common. Practising health professionals are constantly placed in situations that require them to examine both personal and professional consciences in a multitude of areas. What, for example, should a nurse do when asked to participate in a health procedure that he or she morally objects to or disagrees with? What about the massage therapist who is a single parent and struggling financially? How should he respond if asked by a client to perform "extra" services for triple the pay of a therapeutic massage? And then there's the paramedic who is the first on the scene of a violent car crash. How does she handle the lone survivor's request to let him die, after he is told that his wife and child did not survive?

Ethical debate in the field of the health sciences is, of course, not new. Some ethical debates are commonplace and have been discussed and publicized endlessly in schools, colleges, and universities; discussions of whether a fetus should be considered a life or not and the controversies surrounding requests for assisted death or suicide are two such examples. As technology continues to progress, however, health care institutions face increasingly longer, and newer, lists of ethical scenarios to debate. Modern technology now has the ability to screen developing fetuses for certain birth defects, and with the option to abort in such circumstances evolves a growing concern over a renewal in eugenicist thinking. With rapid technological growth in the areas of the health sciences, the need to find solutions to new ethical dilemmas posed by these very advancements becomes timely and pressing. Predictably, then, it appears that ethics dialogue will play an increasingly important role in the future of health care institutions. It is a demanding time as health care institutions prepare for a possible reinvention of approaches and attitudes toward life, death, and quality of life. This, along with the limited resources faced by many health care facilities and the increased workloads and greater responsibilities of the practitioners themselves, makes ethics dialogue an increasingly important aspect of health care.

The fact that most college and university health sciences programs require students to take an ethics course, as well as the abundance of textbooks in this area of study, suggests that an understanding of ethics as it relates to health sciences is mandatory for the individual intent on a health sciences career. Ethics dialogue continues beyond the confines of the classroom, however, as, once in the workplace, licensed health professionals in Canada are required to uphold and abide by the Code of Ethics for their particular professions in order to preserve patient rights and dignity.

ETHICAL PRINCIPLES IN HEALTH CARE

As mentioned previously, ethical principles are guidelines that help us navigate the complexities of ethical decision-making by providing a template for model behaviour. The need for ethical guidelines in medical practice has long been recognized as evidenced by creation of the **Hippocratic Oath** (see Box 6.1), a document that set the standards for ethical medical practice in the fourth century. Today, modernized versions of this ancient document (see Box 6.2) are still used around the world to provide a framework for ethical behaviour. Once you have looked at both versions of the oath, answer the questions that follow each document.

BOX 6.1

The Hippocratic Oath (Classical Version)

I SWEAR by Apollo the physician, and Aesculapius, and Health, and All-heal, and all the gods and goddesses, that, according to my ability and judgment, I will keep this Oath and this stipulation—to reckon him who taught me this Art equally dear to me as my parents, to share my substance with him, and relieve his necessities if required; to look upon his offspring in the same footing as my own brothers, and to teach them this art, if they shall wish to learn it, without fee or stipulation; and that by precept, lecture, and every other mode of instruction, I will impart a knowledge of the Art to my own sons, and those of my teachers, and to disciples bound by a stipulation and oath according to the law of medicine, but to none others. I will follow that system of regimen which, according to my ability and judgment, I consider for the benefit of my patients, and abstain from whatever is deleterious and mischievous. I will give no deadly medicine to any one if asked, nor suggest any such counsel; and in like manner I will not give to a woman a pessary to produce abortion. With purity and with holiness I will pass my life and practice my Art. I will not cut persons laboring under the stone, but will leave this to be done by men who are practitioners of this work. Into whatever houses I enter, I will go into them for the benefit of the sick, and will abstain from every voluntary act of mischief and corruption; and, further from the seduction of females or males, of freemen and slaves. Whatever, in connection with my professional practice or not, in connection with it, I see or hear, in the life of men, which ought not to be spoken of abroad, I will not divulge, as reckoning that all such should be kept secret. While I continue to keep this Oath unviolated, may it be granted to me to enjoy life and the practice of the art, respected by all men, in all times! But should I trespass and violate this Oath, may the reverse be my lot!

Source: The Oath, *by Hippocrates, ca. 400 B.C.E. (Francis Adams, Trans.). Retrieved from http://classics. mit.edu/Hippocrates/hippooath.html*

Discussion Questions:

1. Work individually or in groups to rewrite the classical version of the Hippocratic Oath for modern audience.

2. Does the classical Oath reflect the complexities of the modern health care system? Why or why not?

BOX 6.2

The Hippocratic Oath (Modern Version)

I swear to fulfill, to the best of my ability and judgment, this covenant:

I will respect the hard-won scientific gains of those physicians in whose steps I walk, and gladly share such knowledge as is mine with those who are to follow.

I will apply, for the benefit of the sick, all measures [that] are required, avoiding those twin traps of overtreatment and therapeutic nihilism.

I will remember that there is art to medicine as well as science, and that warmth, sympathy, and understanding may outweigh the surgeon's knife or the chemist's drug.

I will not be ashamed to say "I know not," nor will I fail to call in my colleagues when the skills of another are needed for a patient's recovery.

I will respect the privacy of my patients, for their problems are not disclosed to me that the world may know. Most especially must I tread with care in matters of life and death. If it is given me to save a life, all thanks. But it may also be within my power to take a life; this awesome responsibility must be faced with great humbleness and awareness of my own frailty. Above all, I must not play at God.

I will remember that I do not treat a fever chart, a cancerous growth, but a sick human being, whose illness may affect the person's family and economic stability. My responsibility includes these related problems, if I am to care adequately for the sick.

I will prevent disease whenever I can, for prevention is preferable to cure.

I will remember that I remain a member of society, with special obligations to all my fellow human beings, those sound of mind and body as well as the infirm.

If I do not violate this oath, may I enjoy life and art, respected while I live and remembered with affection thereafter. May I always act so as to preserve the finest traditions of my calling and may I long experience the joy of healing those who seek my help.

Source: "Hippocratic oath: Modern version," by Louis Lasagna, 1964.

Discussion Questions:

1. Contrast the modern Hippocratic Oath with the classical version. How are the two different?

2. Is there anything in the modern Oath that is missing or that you would like to see included?

Power imbalances lay the foundation for many ethical challenges, and it is virtually impossible to find a profession where hierarchy and power imbalances do not exist to some extent. In health care, such power imbalances are obvious when one observes the doctor–nurse relationship or even the nurse–patient relationship. Given such imbalances of power, as well as the complexity and frequency of life-determining decisions that health care workers must engage in daily, principles that establish a foundation for helping us determine the best course of action in the face of ethically difficult situations are vital. In the following section, you will be introduced to eight such principles. These principles extend across the health care spectrum and are used, in varying guises, as base guidelines for ethical behaviour in many health professions, including nursing, paramedics, physiotherapy, massage therapy, and occupational therapy. These principles, or variations of them, are usually encrypted within a specific profession's Code of Ethics.

1) Autonomy

The principle of autonomy lies at the core of patient rights. Autonomy refers to the right of patients to have a say in all aspects of their personal care: who treats them, how they are treated, and what treatments they choose to undergo or decline. The notion of *coercion* must also be considered in any discussion of patient autonomy. A caregiver must not attempt to force or coerce a patient into making particular health decisions. Rather, the caregiver must preserve patient autonomy by thoroughly and honestly informing the patient of pertinent matters related to his or her health and treatments so that well-informed health decisions can be made by either the patient or those acting on the patient's behalf. The current emphasis on patient *voice* contrasts with the traditional paternalistic model of health care, which assumed expert opinion on the part of the caregiver, oftentimes compromising patient autonomy in the process.

Ethical dilemmas and challenges to the patient's autonomy happen frequently in the health care workplace. For example, a patient may assert his or her right to smoke cigarettes despite a serious lung condition. Here, the ethical dilemma for the caregiver becomes one of respecting the patient's right to smoke while at the same time trying to protect the patient from physical harm that might result from his or her right to smoke.

The consent form is used by health care institutions to assure autonomy in cases of surgery or other risky treatments. Common categories of consent are explained below.

Implied Consent:
This occurs when a patient consents through words, behaviour, or circumstance. If a patient opens his or her mouth for the purposes of thermometer insertion, this would be considered implied consent through behaviour.

Express Consent:
This refers to written or verbal consent, and is usually required when intervention is painful or risky. See the sample express consent form in Box 6.3.

BOX 6.3 | **Consent Form**

Consent to investigation, treatment, or operative procedure

(1) I, _____ , hereby consent to undergo the investigation, treatment or operative procedure _____ , ordered by or to be performed by Dr._____.

(2) The nature and anticipated effect of what is proposed including the significant risks and alternatives available have been explained to me. I am satisfied with these explanations and I have understood them.

(3) I also consent to such additional or alternative investigations, treatments, or operative procedures as in the opinion of Dr._____ are immediately necessary.

(4) I further agree that in his or her discretion, Dr._____ may make use of the assistance of other surgeons, physicians, and hospital medical staff (including trainees) and may permit them to order or perform all or part of the investigation, treatment, or operative procedure, and I agree that they shall have the same discretion in my investigation and treatment as Dr. _____.

Dated_____

day / month / year

Witness_____

Patient_____

Source: From Consent: A guide for canadian physicians *(4th Edition), by Kenneth G. Evans and Gowling Lafeur Henderson LLP, 2006, May, Ottawa: Canadian Medical Protective Association. Retrieved from http://www.cmpa-acpm.ca/cmpapdo4/docs/resource_files/ml_guides/consent_guide/com_cg_basicelements-e.cfm. Reprinted with permission.*

Advanced Directives:

An advanced directive falls under the category of express consent and is a written document that expresses how a patient desires to be dealt with in an end-of-life or crisis situation in the event that he or she is incapable of making his or her own health decisions. Advanced directives may involve specific directions on how to handle an end-of-life decision, or they may simply authorize a specific individual to act on the patient's behalf to make such a decision. See the sample advanced directives form in Box 6.4.

BOX 6.4 | **The Advanced Directives Form**

Health Care Directive

Please type or print legibly

Manitoba

This is the Health Care Directive of:

Name _____

Address _____ City _____

Province _____ Postal Code _____ Telephone ( ) _____

Part 1 – Designation of a Health Care Proxy

You may name one or more persons who will have the power to make decisions about your medical treatment when you lack the ability to make those decisions yourself. If you do not wish to name a proxy, you may skip this part.

I hereby designate the following person(s) as my Health Care Proxy:

Proxy 1

Name _____

Address _____

_____

City _____

Province _____ Postal Code _____

Telephone ( ) _____

Proxy 2

Name _____

Address _____

_____

City _____

Province _____ Postal Code _____

Telephone ( ) _____

(Check ✔ one choice only.) For an explanation of "consecutively" and "jointly" please see the reverse side of this form).

If I have named more than one proxy, I wish them to act:
❏ **consecutively** OR ❏ **jointly**

My Health Care Proxy may make medical decisions on my behalf when I lack the capacity to do so for myself (*check ✔ one choice only*):

❏ With **no restrictions**

❏ With **restrictions as follows:**

_____

_____

_____

_____

Part 2 – Treatment Instructions

In this part, you may set out your instructions concerning medical treatment that you do or do not wish to receive and the circumstances in which you do or do not wish to receive that treatment. REMEMBER – your instructions can only be carried out if they are set out clearly and precisely. If you do not wish to provide any treatment instructions, you may skip this part.

_____

_____

_____

_____

_____

Part 3 – Signature and Date

You must sign and date this Health Care Directive. No witness is required.

Signature _____

Date _____

If you are unable to sign yourself, a substitute may sign on your behalf. The substitute must sign in your presence and in the presence of a witness. The proxy or the proxy's spouse cannot be the substitute or witness.

Name of substitute: _____

Address _____

_____

Signature _____

Date _____

Name of witness: _____

Address _____

_____

Signature _____

Date _____

MG-3506 (Rev. 05/04)

Source: From Health Care Directive, *by Government of Manitoba, 2004. Retrieved from http://www.gov.mb.ca/ health/documents/hcd.pdf. Reprinted with permission.*

Discussion Questions:

The following questions are based on the sample express consent and advanced directives forms found, respectively, in Boxes 6.3 and 6.4. Work in groups.

1. What does the term *proxy* mean in the advanced directives form?

2. The advanced directives form distinguishes between acting "consecutively" and "jointly" in the event of more than one proxy. How are these two actions different?

3. The advanced directives form excludes a proxy or proxy's wife from being called as a substitute or witness. Why do you think this is the case?

4. Do these two forms adhere to the requirements of good writing as demonstrated by COCOACAT? Where, for example, does the advanced directive form particularly emphasize the need for clarity and conciseness? Why?

5. Do you think the two forms fulfill their overall purposes? You may need to revisit pp. 145–146 where the purpose of each form is presented. Is there anything you think should be added to either form? If so, what and why?

6. Determine how each form reflects, in content and intent, the eight ethical principles discussed in this chapter: autonomy, preservation of life, beneficence, non-maleficence, veracity or truth-telling, confidentiality, privacy, and fidelity.

2) Preservation of life

The underlying tenet inherent in this second principle is that everything possible must be done in order to preserve the well-being and, ultimately, the life of a patient. While this appears to be self-evident, the preservation of life principle can become quite complicated in the realities of the health care workplace in the face of the following questions: What is the definition of life? Should life be defined in purely technical terms, or should it be defined more broadly in terms of quality? If it is determined that an individual can never have quality of life, should that life be preserved? Who determines what quality of life is? Canadian courts know all too well how complex issues relating to the quality of life can get. In the famous 1993 Latimer case, Robert Latimer took the life of his daughter Tracy, determining that she had no quality of life because of her cerebral palsy. Court documents, however, paint a picture of a young girl who smiled and appeared enthusiastic in her interactions with others. Despite these smiles, Robert Latimer determined that his daughter had no quality of life and suffocated and gassed her to death, citing mercy and his daughter's lack of quality of life as his defence (CBC News, "'Compassionate Homicide,'" Dec. 6, 2010).

Health care workers may, indeed, find themselves confronting situations related to the controversies surrounding definitions of *quality of life*. A patient may, for example, resist life-saving procedures, feeling he or she has no quality of life. Such wishes or requests become a dilemma for the health care worker who is supposed to assist in the preservation of life.

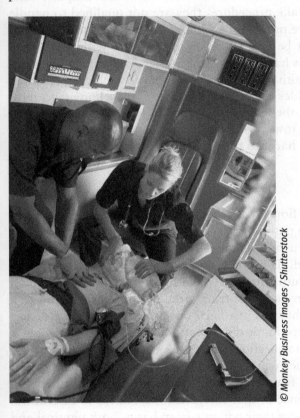
© Monkey Business Images / Shutterstock

3) Beneficence

The principle of beneficence requires caregivers to act beneficently or in ways that benefit their patients and do not produce harm. As well, caregivers must act as advocates for vulnerable patients who cannot "speak" for themselves. In fact, communities come to expect beneficent care from their caregivers, and their faith in the medical system centres around this expectation. An ethical dilemma relating to the principle of beneficence might present itself in the case of paramedic dispatch to an attempted suicide. At such a scene, a paramedic may find him- or herself having to perform life-saving procedures on a patient who wants to die. Here, patient autonomy, in this case the patient's desire to die, clashes with the paramedic's obligation to aid and resuscitate the ill.

4) Non-maleficence

In ethical literature, refraining from knowingly harming patients is referred to as non-maleficence. Related to the principle of beneficence, which requires that caregivers protect patients from harm, non-maleficence demands that caregivers should not knowingly cause or inflict harm on their patients. In upholding this principle, caregivers are required to practise and provide information only within the scope of their specialties and not perform or undertake procedures they are not qualified to handle because of potential harm. Health care professionals know all too well, however, that temporarily harming a patient cannot be avoided when medications with side effects or other uncomfortable manifestations have to be administered. The principle of non-maleficence is often challenged in health care. One such scenario includes providing a patient with medication that provides pain relief but that is also known to have addictive properties. In this situation, the health care provider is caught between two ethical principles: acting beneficently toward the patient by working to decrease the patient's pain, and not causing future harm to the patient through the administration of an addictive drug.

5) Veracity or truth-telling

In any relationship, a commitment to honesty is crucial. In the patient–caregiver relationship, this is also the case because patient trust forms the cornerstone for patient well-being. If patients do not have trusting relationships with their caregivers, their healing process may be compromised. The potential challenges of veracity become apparent in situations where "the truth hurts." A health care provider might find him- or herself in a situation where revelation of truth would cause great distress to a patient. If, for example, a young mother has just been taken into intensive care after a serious car accident in which her six-month-old infant did not survive, how does a health care team member respond if she questions her child's whereabouts? Should the child's death be disclosed to the mother who is currently experiencing great physical distress? The ethical dilemma arising from this situation involves a conflict between the principles of veracity and beneficence in that caregivers must strive to be truthful toward their patients but also to preserve their patients from harm, both physical and psychological. The principle of veracity extends beyond the confines of the patient–caregiver relationship and includes relationships among the caregivers themselves. Providers must be honest in their dealing with colleagues and managers and must not engage in fraud or cover-up.

6) Confidentiality and privacy

Many workplaces, like banks and police stations, store sensitive client information. Similarly, the health care provider has access to a variety of sensitive patient information that includes a client's medical and psychological history, all of which must remain confidential. Not revealing the contents of sensitive documents is one thing; retaining privacy in day-to-day interactions with a patient is another. On a day-to-day basis, caregivers are involved intimately with patients in their roles of feeding, bathing, and dressing them. They may witness them crying or screaming; during visiting hours, they see the stresses inherent in patients' personal relationships. The patient is entitled to privacy throughout all these encounters: curtains should be drawn when performing private procedures and assessments, and the patient's body should always be treated with dignity. In cases where patient health data requires disclosure, written approval is usually necessary. A dilemma that can arise from upholding the principle of confidentiality and privacy is the situation where a patient has, in confidence, revealed life-threatening information to a caregiver. The caregiver now has an ethical dilemma in determining whether to violate the principle of confidentiality in order to preserve the principle of beneficence, if she feels withholding this information could compromise the patient's, or others', health in any way.

The opinion piece in Box 6.5, "Royal Hospital Scandal Shows Patient Privacy Is a Matter of Ethics," reinforces the importance of patient confidentiality. The reflection activity afterwards is a good opportunity to think about the various implications of confidentiality breaches in health care.

| BOX 6.5 | **Royal Hospital Scandal Shows Patient Privacy Is a Matter of Ethics** |

Can we please stop describing the efforts of two Australian DJs to get the scoop on the state of Kate Middleton's pregnancy as a hoax or a prank?

The actions of the 2Day FM duo, however sophomoric, were a clear attempt to obtain confidential medical information about a hospital patient, and they used subterfuge—impersonation even—to do so.

This was not a laughing matter, even without the tragic twist we know all too well, the suicide of nurse Jacintha Saldanha.

Medical files, whether they pertain to a princess or a pauper, are private, and we have a host of ethical, administrative and legislative provisions to protect the information.

That a patient's privacy was so easily breached by a couple of buffoons should lead us to ponder the challenges of handling health information properly. Tremendous pressures exist in the health system to make information easily accessible to facilitate care, while respecting individual patients' inalienable right to privacy.

While there should be no shame in undergoing medical treatment, the reality is that there is stigma associated with many medical conditions and treatments. People want to

continued

keep information secret to prevent everything from losing jobs to messing up relationships. Delicate issues can appear in a medical file: an abortion, a sexually transmitted disease, treatment for psychiatric illness, a history of drug use and so on.

Privacy is not a new concern. Confidentiality has been a concern since the advent of medicine. The Hippocratic oath—dating from the fifth century—reads: "I will respect the privacy of my patients, for their problems are not disclosed to me that the world may know." This oath is sworn by physicians and other health-care professionals, but living up to it can be a challenge. Health workers are human; there is a temptation for some to snoop. Just last week, an employee of Vancouver Coastal Health was fired for accessing the health records of five media personalities out of curiosity. In 2007, after Hollywood actor George Clooney crashed his motorcycle in upstate New York, 40 employees at the hospital where he was treated were suspended for peeking at his file, and some even sold information to tabloids.

There are concerns that the move to electronic health records will make it easier to violate privacy, but these cases demonstrate that the opposite is true. The benefit of computerized records is that you can create privacy settings and track access, something that is impossible with paper files.

For other matters, protocols are in place. But put yourself in the shoes of the nurse or doctor who fields a call from a family member desperate for news on a loved one. Nobody wants to sound like a petty bureaucrat, whether they are taking a call from the Queen or from a distraught mom.

More concerning are the more nefarious attempts to violate privacy by insurers, employers, private investigators, police and current/ex-lovers.

This was such a problem in the late 1970s that Ontario established the Commission of Inquiry into the Confidentiality of Health Information, headed by Mr. Justice Horace Krever (who would later head the inquiry on tainted blood).

It revealed a litany of inappropriate behaviour, including OHIP employees acting as double agents for private insurers (who used the information to deny claims), health workers selling medical files to insurers, employers and divorce lawyers, and police routinely accessing medical files to, among other things, mount smear campaigns against politicians.

Judge Krever made a number of recommendations to clean up the problem, but his overarching conclusion was that new laws were not really needed, what was required was that existing ethical standards and laws be enforced.

That remains true to this day.

In fact, research has shown that the No. 1 reason privacy is breached is health workers looking for dirt on their sexual partners, past and present.

Still, the vast majority of health professionals play by the rules. Yet, a scandal should serve as a reminder that in health care—where patients are vulnerable and their intimacies revealed—trust is essential.

What that means, among other things, is that privacy is sacred and a culture of confidentiality must be the norm.

Source: From "Royal Hospital scandal shows patient privacy is a matter of ethics," by André Picard, 2012, Dec. 13, The Globe and Mail. *Retrieved from http://www.theglobeandmail.com/life/health-and-fitness/health/royal-hospital-scandal-shows-patient-privacy-is-a-matter-of-ethics/article6344222. Reprinted with permission from* The Globe and Mail.

Reflect carefully on the contents of the article "Royal Hospital Scandal Shows Patient Privacy Is a Matter of Ethics," *and then write a thoughtful response to it, commenting on points you feel are most relevant and concerning, especially in relation to the security of health records. In your response, you may want to consider who you feel is at most fault in this scenario and if and how this scenario could be prevented from happening in the future. Consider also how the scenario might differ if the confidentiality breach happened to a non-celebrity. Your instructor may ask you to share your response with the class.*

7) Justice

© khz / Shutterstock

Justice refers to the principle of fairness that should operate in an ideal society. Justice implies that everyone is entitled to the same level of care and consideration in terms of distribution of resources, access to resources, and so on. The realm of just treatment becomes challenging in a world where health care resources are scarce and the health care provider often has little input in administrative decision-making locally, provincially, and beyond. While Canada's public health care system reflects justice, in theory, with its emphasis on universality and accessibility, inequities still occur, with some people being unable to afford expenses not covered by provincial health plans. Justice as it relates to health care can be divided into two types: *distributive justice* and *complimentary justice*.

Distributive justice:

This type of justice demands that resources and taxation be distributed fairly and properly. It also demands equality of treatment in terms of sex, race, economic class, and the like.

I remember seeing a story on the news about a man in Winnipeg who died while waiting for treatment in a hospital ER room. He was in the ER room for 34 hours! No one approached him this entire time. I can't help but think the fact that he was Aboriginal and unkempt played a role in his lack of treatment. What is really disgusting is that he was in the ER for a treatable bladder infection. A security guard said he thought he was intoxicated and just sleeping it off. Talk about stereotyping. To this day, I can't get this story out of my mind. I have vowed to myself that when I graduate from nursing in two years, no one ever be ignored under my watch, especially the most vulnerable. He was also a double amputee so probably didn't have much mobility to approach the staff. It doesn't matter. Someone should have approached him in 34 hours. Would this have happened to a tall, white man in a business suit?

—Bachelor of Nursing student

Compensatory justice:

This type of justice refers to the recognition of harm and the responsibility of just societies to compensate individuals for wrongdoing.

A challenge that might arise relating to the principle of justice includes the knowledge of unequal treatment. Perhaps a nurse has noticed that the doctor for whom she works treats his white patients better than his oriental patients. The nurse finds herself facing an ethical challenge as she is required by her profession to uphold the principle of justice, which calls for the equal treatment of all, but at the same time she is reluctant to get into hot water with her superior, who has more professional power than she does and with whom she must work on a daily basis.

8) Fidelity

The principle of fidelity demands behaviour that demonstrates loyalty and faithfulness toward patients. As such, this principle summarizes many of the expectations inherent in several of the principles already mentioned. Above all, this principle requires caregivers to uphold with integrity the responsibilities that result from their designations as licensed health care providers. This principle also includes the expectation that contracts be respected and honoured. If a patient agrees to a procedure, the doers of that procedure have the obligation to conduct that procedure professionally and properly. Challenges in the area of fidelity are numerous in the health care workplace. One example would be the nurse who is required to assist in an abortion procedure when she herself does not believe in abortion. In this situation, the nurse's fidelity to her profession is challenged by her personal beliefs.

> *It's always difficult when family members want you to keep resuscitating a patient even when you know such efforts are fruitless. I've had to do all sorts of crazy things, and I mean crazy, just to appease family members who are not ready to let their loved ones go. Sometimes, because family members are not ready to deal with loss, they want us to keep putting the patient through excruciating pain and discomfort. This seems selfish to me. Love also means "letting go."*
>
> —RPN (hospital)

TRY IT YOURSELF

What ethical principle is being questioned or asserted in each of the following scenarios? Some scenarios might reflect more than one principle.

1. A patient no longer wants to live and asks that he no longer be resuscitated.

2. A massage therapist who has a family wedding to attend on the weekend has been asked by her manager to work overtime on the same weekend.

3. A paramedic team having coffee at Tim Hortons openly discusses the health of a local celebrity they just transported to the hospital.

4. A patient wants a second opinion on her health diagnosis.

5. A nurse offers to sit with a patient on his lunch break because he sees that the patient is distressed.

6. A patient does not come for his regular medical checkups because he cannot afford the transit to get to the hospital.

7. A nurse speaks to her manager about concerns she has regarding lack of staffing in her ward.

8. A nurse knows that the husband of one of her patients is having an affair with another nurse on the ward.

9. A patient rejects a life-saving blood transfusion on religious grounds.

10. A patient is distressed about an upcoming surgery. The nurse tells the patient, "Dr. Harris is the best. You'll come out of the surgery feeling like you're twenty years old."

THE CODE OF ETHICS DOCUMENT

Now that you have been introduced to common ethical principles in health care, it is time to look specifically at one very important document, the Code of Ethics.

Most health professionals in Canada are required to abide by a code that sets the behavioural standard for their particular profession. Mostly, such documents outline the values and intentions of a profession, state the obligations that professionals within that occupation have to those in their care, and provide a base for determining proper conduct in ethically challenging or complex situations. Overall, the Code of Ethics document is meant to inspire consistent, professional conduct and provide a tool for ethically sound decision making. Because these documents are, generally, available to the public, they also underscore the need for transparency and accountability within a profession. Code of Ethics documents must also undergo regular revision. The revision process is important, not only in terms of acknowledging occupational change, but also in the way it provides the opportunity for collegial reflection and information sharing.

Code of Ethics documents do not necessarily supply all the answers, especially in very complex scenarios, but they do lay a strong foundation for ethically sound and responsible decision making. Workers that violate the principles of a given code face consequences that could include job loss or legal action, so adherence to the parameters of a given Code is absolutely essential.

It is important to note that even if a health workplace does not have an official Code of Ethics document, workers must still act ethically and honourably in order to uphold the standards of their professions and the dignity of their patients.

Below you will find actual Canadian Code of Ethics documents for five health professions: nurses (Box 6.6), paramedics (Box 6.7), physiotherapists (Box 6.8), pharmacists (Box 6.9), and funeral services (Box 6.10). Work in groups to discuss the Code of Ethics for your desired profession. Specifically, try to think of one workplace scenario that demonstrates, and one that challenges, each point in the code you are working with.

Example:

Point 1 in Code of Ethics for Registered Nurses (providing safe, compassionate, competent, and ethical care)

Demonstration:

- a nurse who gives her patient medication that causes drowsiness, and who therefore makes sure her patient is carefully monitored and/or assisted when getting out of bed or going to the bathroom in order to prevent further harm in the form of fall or injury

Challenge:

- a nurse who is negligent in documenting a significant change in a patient's chart

BOX 6.6   Code of Ethics for Registered Nurses

1. Providing safe, compassionate, competent, and ethical care
2. Promoting health and well-being
3. Promoting and respecting informed decision-making
4. Preserving dignity
5. Maintaining privacy and confidentiality
6. Promoting justice
7. Being accountable . . .

Source: ©Canadian Nurses Association. Reprinted with permission. Further reproduction prohibited.

BOX 6.7   Code of Ethics for Paramedics (Manitoba)

The Paramedic Association of Manitoba affirms its responsibility to develop the spirit of professionalism within its membership and to promote high ethical standards in the practice of Emergency Medical Services.

Paramedic Association of Manitoba members are committed to achieving excellence:

I. The paramedic shall regard their responsibility to the patient as paramount and strive to preserve human life, alleviate suffering, and adhere to the principles of beneficence. The paramedic must have respect for their patients' autonomy and ensure quality and equal availability of care to all.

II. The paramedic shall provide services based on human need, with respect for human dignity, unrestricted by consideration of age, race, sex, color, status, national or ethnic origin, or physical/mental disability.

III. The paramedic shall respect, protect, and fulfill the commitment to confidentiality of patient information in accordance with law.

IV. The paramedic shall practice their profession uninfluenced by motives of profit.

V. The paramedic will assume all responsibility for his or her actions, and ensure that others receive credit for their work and contributions.

continued

VI. The paramedic assumes responsibility to expose incompetence or unethical conduct of others to the appropriate authority. The paramedic refuses to participate in unethical procedures.

VII. Each practitioner understands and complies with the laws and regulations relevant to their professional role.

VIII. The paramedic shall participate in defining and upholding standards of professional practice and education. The paramedic strives for professional excellence by maintaining competence in knowledge and skills necessary to provide quality care and maintaining currency in issues related to EMS.

IX. The paramedic recognizes a responsibility to participate in professional activities, associations, and research that contribute to the improvement of public health, and will and [sic] encourage the participation of peers.

This code of ethics is not law, but a professional standard of conduct which defines the essentials of honorable behaviour for the paramedic; a behaviour that will foster pride, admiration, and respect for the profession of paramedicine.

Source: From Code of ethics, *by Paramedic Association of Manitoba, 2013. Retrieved from http://www .paramedicsofmanitoba.ca/index.php/about/code. Courtesy of the Paramedic Association of Manitoba.*

BOX 6.8 **Code of Ethics for Physiotherapists**

Premise:

The provision of effective quality care, while respecting the rights of the client, shall be the primary consideration of each member of the profession.

Responsibilities to the Client

1. Physiotherapists shall respect the client's rights, dignity, needs, wishes and values.

2. Physiotherapists may not refuse care to any client on grounds of race, religion, ethnic or national origin, age, sex, sexual orientation, and social or health status.

3. Physiotherapists must respect the client's or surrogate's right to be informed about the effects of treatment and inherent risks.

4. Physiotherapists must give clients or surrogates the opportunity to consent to or decline treatment or alterations in the treatment regime.

5. Physiotherapists shall confine themselves to clinical diagnosis and management in those aspects of physiotherapy in which they have been educated and which are recognized by

the profession. (Physiotherapists are responsible for recognizing and practising within their levels of competence. The clinical diagnosis is established by taking a history and conducting a physical and functional examination. The identification of the client's problems and the physiotherapeutic management is based on this diagnosis in conjunction with an understanding of pertinent biopsychosocial factors. This rule does not restrict the expansion of the scope of physiotherapy practice.)

6. Physiotherapists shall assume full responsibility for all care they provide.

7. Physiotherapists shall not treat clients when the medical diagnosis or clinical condition indicates that the commencement or continuation of physiotherapy is not warranted or is contraindicated.

8. Physiotherapists shall request consultation with, or refer clients to, colleagues or members of other health professions when, in the opinion of the physiotherapist, such action is in the best interest of the client.

9. Physiotherapists shall document the client's history and relevant subjective information, the physiotherapist's objective findings, clinical diagnosis, treatment plan and procedures, explanation to the client, progress notes and discharge summary.

10. Physiotherapists shall respect all client information as confidential. Such information shall not be communicated to any person without the consent of the client or surrogate except when required by law.

11. Physiotherapists, with the client's or surrogate's consent, may delegate specific aspects of the care of that client to a person deemed by the physiotherapist to be competent to carry out the care safely and effectively.

12. Physiotherapists are responsible for all duties they delegate to personnel under their supervision.

Source: From Responsibilities to the client: Rules of conduct, *by Canadian Physiotherapy Association, 1988. Retrieved from http://www.physiotherapy.ca. Canadian Physiotherapy Association, Responsibilities to the client: Rules of Conduct, 1988.*

BOX 6.9   **Code of Ethics for Pharmacists (BC)**

Code of Ethics (Values)

All pharmacists practicing in British Columbia are governed by a Code of Ethics. By entering the profession of pharmacy, every pharmacist commits to moral norms of conduct. We assume a professional commitment to the health and well being of every one of our patients.

Value 1
A pharmacist respects the professional relationship with the patient and acts with honesty, integrity and compassion.

continued

Value 2
A pharmacist honours the individual needs, values and dignity of the patient.

Value 3
A pharmacist supports the right of the patient to make personal choices about pharmacy care.

Value 4
A pharmacist provides competent care to the patient and actively supports the patient's right to receive competent and ethical health care.

Value 5
A pharmacist protects the patient's right of confidentiality.

Value 6
A pharmacist respects the values and abilities of colleagues and other health professionals.

Value 7
A pharmacist endeavours to ensure that the practice environment contributes to safe and effective pharmacy care.

Value 8
A pharmacist ensures continuity of care in the event of job action, pharmacy closure or conflict with moral beliefs.

Source: From "Code of Ethics (Values)," by College of Pharmacists of British Columbia, 2013. Retrieved from http://www.bcpharmacists.org/legislation_standards/standards_of_practice/code_of_ethics_values).php. Courtesy of the College of Pharmacists of British Columbia.

BOX 6.10 | Code of Ethical Practices (Ontario Funeral Services Association)

22.01 Every Member shall observe the following code (the "Code of Ethical Practices") and shall if requested provide assurances to the Association (referred to in the Code of Ethical Practices as OFSA) that every person, firm, partnership or corporation which the Member represents shall likewise observe the Code.

22.02 The Code of Ethical Practices is as follows:

1. OFSA members are committed to the highest standards of professional service and will serve with care and compassion while respecting all people.
2. OFSA members always conduct themselves professionally and in a manner which promotes the reputation of the funeral service profession and the OFSA.

3. OFSA members observe the requirements of the applicable legislation, and the spirit and letter of this Code of Ethical Practices.
4. OFSA members provide their services to all who request them, without discrimination of any kind.
5. OFSA members keep confidential all personal information given to them.
6. OFSA members always present information outlining the full range of services and products available.
7. OFSA members clearly and accurately describe and document the services and products selected, their related costs, and the terms of payment.
8. OFSA members' fees are commensurate with the services and products provided and are based on known costs of providing them.
9. OFSA members clearly explain legal or other requirements related to embalming and other aspects of funeral arrangements and the options available.
10. OFSA members retain the right to modify and adapt their services to ensure the safety of the public and of their employees and will clearly communicate information regarding any required modifications or adaptations.

Source: From Ontario Funeral Service Association By-Law No. 1, *2012. Retrieved from http://www.ofsa.org/2012_OFSA _By-Law_Consolidation_final.pdf. Reprinted with permission from the Ontario Funeral Services Association (ofsa.org).*

PRACTICE: ETHICAL DISCUSSIONS

You have now had a chance to review and analyze several Code of Ethics documents. Based on your knowledge of the various codes, work in groups to discuss appropriate responses to each of the scenarios below. Be prepared to justify your responses and decisions using the relevant Code of Ethics.

Case 1: The Negligent Colleague

Rosalind Gonzales and Hema Bannerjee are both experienced registered nurses. They have been working together in the same hospital for 15 years. In addition to being long-time colleagues, Gonzales and Bannerjee are also good friends. They socialize frequently, and three years ago Gonzales lent Bannerjee a significant sum of money for an important car repair.

Recently, Bannerjee has become concerned about Gonzales's professional conduct. Gonzales, a normally professional, competent, and popular nurse with the patients, has started to look tired and arrives late to work. Bannerjee noticed Gonzales tripping while wheeling a patient down the hall the other day, and today she is sure that she smelled alcohol on her colleague's breath in the lunch cafeteria. She has also noticed that Gonzales has been negligent in some of her charting duties. In fact, Bannerjee herself has had to approach Gonzales on more than one occasion this week concerning some vague and confusing notations made on a shared patient's chart. Bannerjee is starting to worry that her friend and colleague may be an alcoholic.

Discussion questions:

1. What ethical principle or principles are at play here?

2. What specific ethical challenge or challenges does Bannerjee face?

3. What would you do in this situation? Justify your response.

4. Based on the Code of Ethics for nurses, what should Bannerjee do in this situation? Justify your response.

Case 2: The Abusive Patient

Saba Hassan is a physiotherapist who was just recently hired at a popular community health clinic. Because she is a new employee at the clinic, she is under intense scrutiny and must serve a one-year probation period. Hassan loves her job and looks forward to seeing her patients and monitoring their progress. For the past week, however, she has felt anxious in having to deal with one particular patient: Horatio Littleton. Littleton, who is healing from a broken leg, comes for therapy three times a week. So far, Littleton has made several sexual comments about Hassan's body and has tried to grope her while she was helping him with his leg exercises. Hassan finds his inappropriate behaviour highly distressing. Hassan has noticed that she is short and abrasive when interacting with Littleton, and shakes with anxiety prior to treating him.

Discussion questions:

1. What ethical principle or principles are at play here?

2. What specific ethical challenge or challenges does Hassan face?

3. What would you do in this situation? Justify your response.

4. Based on the Code of Ethics for physiotherapists, what should Hassan do? Justify your response.

Case 3: The Grateful Patient

Paramedic Lucien Godbout and his ambulance partner James Pauley have just arrived at the apartment building of an elderly gentleman who called 911 complaining of a fall and a broken hip. Upon arrival, Godbout and Pauley examine the patient and conclude the patient's self-assessment is correct: he has a broken hip. The two paramedics strap the patient onto a stretcher in order to transport him to the ambulance downstairs. As they are exiting the apartment, the patient thrusts a $100 bill into Godbout's hands. "You remind me so much of my son," he says. "Here, take this, I might not see you again. You have been so nice."

Discussion questions:

1. What ethical principle or principles are at play here?

2. What specific ethical challenge or challenges does Godbout face?

3. What would you do in this situation? Justify your response.

4. Based on the Code of Ethics for paramedics, what should Godbout do? Justify your response.

Case 4: The Abused Patient

Tatiana Gruszinksy is a registered nurse working in the ER department of her local hospital. Gruszinksy is on duty one night when she sees her best friend and her 10-year-old daughter in the waiting room. Gruszinksy ends up being responsible for assessing her friend's daughter before the doctor's arrival. During her examination, she discovers several bruises on the child's body; her extensive professional experience tells her these bruises are the results of physical abuse. Gruszinksy is very distressed by these findings. Her best friend, the child's mother, is attempting to make small talk while the examination is taking place.

Discussion questions:

1. What ethical principle or principles are at play here?

2. What specific ethical challenge or challenges does Gruszinksy face?

3. What would you do in this situation? Justify your response.

4. Based on the Code of Ethics for nurses, what should Gruszinksy do? Justify your response.

Case 5: The Unlikeable Client

Samuel Raine, the director of the Raine Funeral Hume, runs the only funeral home in the small town of Whitley. In the past few years, the town with a population of 450, has experienced significant tragedy. Three women in the town have been raped over a period of five years and, recently, a local, David Lean, confessed his guilt to all three rapes before taking his own life. Leans's parents have been in contact with Raine to discuss funeral arrangements for their son. Raine is considered a leader in the small community and knows the devastation the man's assaults have inflicted on the town and the various families directly involved. He is worried about backlash.

Discussion questions:

1. What ethical principle or principles are at play here?

2. What specific ethical challenge or challenges does Raine face?

3. What would you do in this situation? Justify your response.

4. Based on the Code of Ethical Practices (Ontario Funeral Services Association) what should Raine do? Justify your response.

5. Read the article "Boston Bombing Suspect's Body in Limbo" (Box 6.11). How is the situation in the article similar to the case presented here? How is it different?

| BOX 6.11 | **Boston Bombing Suspect's Body in Limbo** |

There is no standard practice for this situation.

As Boston bombing suspect Tamerlan Tsarnaev's body lies in a Worcester, Mass., funeral home, the question looms: What to do with the corpse of a person suspected of a crime that horrified and terrorized a nation?

Tsarnaev, 26, suspected in the April 15 bombing that killed three people and injured more than 260, died four days later in a shootout with police. His brother, Dzhokhar, is in jail, charged with the bombings.

Tamerlan Tsarnaev's body was rejected by several funeral homes until Graham Putnam & Mahoney agreed to handle the service.

"We take an oath to do this," funeral director Peter Stefan said. "Can I pick and choose? No. Can I separate the sins from the sinners? No."

Protesters gather outside the funeral home.

Stefan has been unable to find a cemetery that would allow the burial. He wants government officials to help.

No, said Gov. Deval Patrick. He said dealing with the body is a "family issue."

City Manager Robert Healy has advised against a burial in the area. He said the city "would be adversely impacted by the turmoil, protests and widespread media presence at such an interment."

Cremation is not an option for a Muslim. The body must be buried underground, said Council on American–Islamic Relations spokeswoman Yasmin Nouh.

Stefan said Monday that Tsarnaev's mother, Zubeidat Tsarnaeva, wants the body returned to Russia, where Tamerlan Tsarnaev was born and where his parents returned after the family lived in Massachusetts.

A Worcester man, William Breault, is trying to raise money to send the body to Russia.

Tsarnaev's uncle, Ruslan Tsarni, has said his nephew should be buried in Massachusetts, where he lived for the past decade.

The situation is particularly heated because Tsarnaev is not thought of as sick or mentally ill like some killers, said James Alan Fox, a criminology professor at Northeastern University in Boston.

People think he's "evil," Fox said, and society "doesn't forgive or forget."

Families of people who committed very public crimes often keep a grave site unmarked to prevent desecration as well as have private ceremonies, he said.

There were private arrangements for Adam Lanza, who killed his mother, 20 Newtown, Conn., schoolchildren and six school staffers, then fatally shot himself, on Dec. 14.

Similarly, Eric Harris, one of the two students who killed 12 classmates and a teacher at Columbine High School in 1999, was buried in a place his parents have not revealed. The other Columbine killer, Dylan Klebold, was cremated.

Osama bin Laden, mastermind of the 9/11 attacks, was buried at sea, his body treated according to Islamic custom, after he was killed in a 2011 raid.

But there are some killers who are in plots with family names, and even some—such as Patrick Henry Sherrill, a U.S. Postal Service employee who killed 14 people in 1986—in a grave with their own name on the gravestone, says Fox.

Source: From "Boston bombing suspect's body in limbo," by Laura Petrecca and Michael Winter, 2013, May 6, USA Today. Retrieved from http://www.usatoday.com/story/news/nation/2013/05/06/uncle-arranging-boston-bomb-suspects-burial-rites/2138277. ©2013 USA Today. Reprinted with permission.

Case 6: The Curious Husband

Belinda Woo is a pharmacist who knows many of her customers well. Recently, Mrs. Davidson, one of her long-time clients, has been coming in for top-ups to her prescription medication. One day her husband, Mr. Davidson, approaches Woo at the pharmacy counter and starts to question the pharmacist about his wife's medication use and the status of her health. Ms. Woo has seen the couple together many times, and they appear to be very happily married.

Discussion questions:

1. What ethical principle or principles are at play here?

2. What specific ethical challenge or challenges does Woo face?

3. What would you do in this situation? Justify your response.

4. Based on the Code of Ethics for Pharmacists (BC), what should Woo do? Justify your response.

CHAPTER LINKS FOR FURTHER EXPLORATION

- **John Dossetor Health Ethics Centre (http://www.bioethics.ualberta.ca/)**

This University of Alberta site promotes engagement and reflection on ethical issues in health care. It provides links to other Canadian ethics sites and has a list of videos on the topic of ethical research in health care.

- **Nova Scotia's Health Ethics Network (http://www.nshen.ca/resource_oe.html)**

On this site, you can find various resources related to ethics in health care, including a video library and readings on a variety of relevant topics including professional boundaries, moral distress and social media and telemedicine.

- **Nursing Services Organization (http://www.nso.com)**

This site offers a legal discussion of nursing malpractice. It also presents case studies, some of which relate to documentation errors, for further analysis and exploration.

TEAMWORK AND PRESENTATION SKILLS

At the end of this chapter, you should be able to

- understand the importance of working in teams in both educational and professional settings
- identify the different roles that are important to the smooth functioning of a team, as well as some of the dysfunctional roles that can interfere with the effectiveness of a team
- identify some strategies for working effectively in teams
- use strategies to overcome presentation anxiety
- prepare and deliver an effective presentation

When I entered the Practical Nursing program, I was completely unprepared for the group presentations we had to do. The first one was a disaster! My group never met face to face, we all tried to do our work independently, and we ended up presenting contradictory and confusing information to the class. We were so nervous while presenting that I don't think anything we said made any sense. Now that I'm working in a hospital, I work in teams all the time and I'm really glad that I had the opportunity to develop some important skills before entering the profession.

—Nurse, Edmonton

INTRODUCTION

While most of this book is concerned with improving your writing skills, there are other important skills, related to writing, that will contribute to your academic and professional success. This chapter will cover two of the most important: teamwork and presentation skills.

In 2006, the Canadian Health Services Research Foundation released a report titled *Teamwork in Healthcare: Promoting Effective Teamwork in Healthcare in Canada*, which concluded that "improved teamwork and collaborative care have been shown to improve performance in many aspects of the healthcare system, including primary healthcare and public health." The report cited research suggesting that "teamwork can significantly reduce workloads; increase job satisfaction and retention; improve patient satisfaction; and reduce patient morbidity" (p. 1). Clinical care in the twenty-first century involves a team of multiple professionals who care for their clients through a process of consultation, communication, and interaction. In order to provide the best possible care, maintain a positive workplace culture, and reduce the likelihood of errors, it is crucial to learn how to work effectively in teams.

Another important skill is the ability to present information orally in front of small or large groups. In addition to daily communication with clients and their families, allied health professionals are often required to make presentations in formal contexts, such as addressing health education topics in the community. Having the skills and confidence to prepare and deliver a presentation will help you be more effective in your job, and will open up opportunities for career advancement.

WORKING IN TEAMS

Although, in the classroom, the sorts of projects we are referring to are often referred to as *groupwork*, we are using the word *team* rather than *group* to highlight the fact that we are not speaking of merely a collection of people, such as a gathering of co-workers waiting for a bus or a crowd of fans at a concert. When we refer to a team, we are referring to a small collection of people who interact with one another in order to achieve common goals. Traditionally, this interaction took place face to face; however, in today's workplace, it is becoming common for teams to connect virtually, by using technology to collaborate.

ROLES IN TEAMS

Belbin's Team Roles

British management theorist Dr. Meredith Belbin spent many years studying teams in action and observed that people in teams tend to assume different roles within the team. Each individual team member has a particular way of behaving in and contributing to the team. He identified nine different roles, which in turn are classified in three categories: Action-Oriented Roles, People-Oriented Roles, and Thought-Oriented Roles. For a list of the nine roles, with their characteristics, please see box 7.1.

BOX 7.1	**Belbin's Team Roles**

ROLE	CHARACTERISTICS
ACTION-ORIENTED ROLES	
The Shaper	Pushes the team to improve, sees challenges as opportunities, suggests possible solutions. Good at motivating the team.
The Implementer	Turns ideas into actions. Organized and efficient. Good at getting things done.
The Completer-Finisher	Ensures that projects are completed on time, with no errors or omissions. Detail-oriented and concerned with deadlines.
PEOPLE-ORIENTED ROLES	
The Coordinator	Assumes the leadership role, identifying the strengths of team members, delegating tasks, and guiding the team.
The Team Worker	Ensures that the team members are working together effectively. Takes on the role of negotiator or mediator. Diplomatic and perceptive.
The Resource Investigator	Explores external resources and contacts on behalf of the team. Outgoing and proactive.
THOUGHT-ORIENTED ROLES	
The Plant	Comes up with new ideas and fresh approaches to solving problems. Often works alone and brings ideas to the team. Creative and innovative.
The Monitor-Evaluator	Analyzes and evaluates the ideas of the team. Weighs all options carefully before making a decision. Objective and insightful.
The Specialist	Possesses specialized knowledge that is necessary for completing the project. Functions as an expert in the area, advising other members of the team.

Source: Adapted from Belbin® team roles, by Belbin Associates, 2012. Retrieved from http://www.belbin.com/rte.asp

The keys to a smoothly functioning team are making sure (1) that the most important roles are covered, and (2) that everyone isn't trying to fill the same role. Think of a hockey team with no goalie, or a basketball team made up of all forwards. We are not saying that every team needs nine members; some team members will fill two or more roles. In addition, people must be allowed to take on roles that come naturally to them. For example, an introvert who prefers to research and come up with ideas on his or her own would be more suited to one of the Thought-Oriented Roles and would be quite uncomfortable, and even ineffective, in an Action-Oriented Role.

Dysfunctional Roles

Just as there are roles that must be filled in order for the team to function successfully, there are also roles that can threaten the team's ability to function. Have you ever known someone who tries to take over every team she is a part of, insisting on having things her way? Or have you ever worked with someone who dismisses every suggestion, saying, "That will never work—we tried it a few years ago and it was a disaster!" For a list of dysfunctional roles and their characteristics, please see Box 7.2.

| BOX 7.2 | **Dysfunctional Roles in Teams** |

ROLE	CHARACTERISTICS
The Bully	...is aggressive, taking control of the team and pushing his or her own interests and goals over those of the team. Often rejects or criticizes others' contributions and refuses to cooperate.
The Downer	...is pessimistic and defeatist, offering reasons that the project will fail.
The Quitter	...is withdrawn and detached from the team, failing to respond to emails and phone calls and saying little in meetings. Denies any responsibility for the outcomes.
The Clown	...refuses to take the project or tasks seriously, and undermines the efforts of the team through the use of inappropriate humour.

BUILDING EFFECTIVE TEAMS

1. Ensure that all the roles are covered by people who possess the necessary skills and strengths for those roles. Let the person with the neatest handwriting take the notes or minutes from meetings. Let the person who loves to speak in public take the lead in oral presentations.

2. Ensure that all team members understand the objectives of the project and demonstrate commitment to them and to the team. Go around the table and have everyone voice their expectations and goals for the project.

3. Encourage open, honest, and respectful communication among the team members. Have a mechanism in place for communication when the team is unable to meet face to face.

4. Elect a leader, and respect the decisions of that individual. It is important to let the leader lead.

5. Have a decision-making process in place from the beginning. Will the team make decisions by consensus (all team members must agree on a solution), or by majority (the team goes with the option with more than half the votes)?

© Adam Gregor / Shutterstock

Think of a time when you worked in a team, either at school or in the workplace. How effectively did the team function? Were all of the important roles covered? Reflect on any conflicts or problems that arose. How could they have been avoided?

Students in Professor Davies's Nursing Practice class have been assigned a team assignment to discuss a case study and present it to the class. They have been given one week to prepare the presentation, and the instructor will take the team members' evaluation of their peers into consideration when assigning a grade.

Ahmad, Nikita, Shantel, Giulia, and Konrad have been put on the same team and given a case to present. They arrange to meet at the coffee shop at noon to begin preparing their assignment. Four of the five members show up on time, but Ahmad is late. After reading over the case, Nikita sighs and says, "I knew it. We got the hardest one. We're never going to be able to understand this case." Konrad says, "This will be challenging, but we can do it. Let's go through the case bit by bit, and then we can figure out how we can best present it to the class." Nikita sighs again. "I hate presentations," she says. "I always get so nervous." Konrad starts reading the case out loud, and Giulia pulls out a piece of paper and writes down ideas as the team members suggest them. After half an hour, Ahmad arrives and asks, "So, what did you guys decide?"

After discussing the case, Konrad suggests that they divide up parts of the case for each member to present. Everyone agrees, and they divide up the parts. Giulia offers to type up her notes and send them to the other team members. Shantel says that they need a schedule of meetings to work on the project. She suggests that they meet twice—once in a few days, and once the day before the presentation, and that they communicate online throughout the week.

Konrad, Giulia, Shantel, and Nikita send each other their ideas and suggestions over the next two days. When it's time to meet, it is clear that Ahmad has not done any work on the project. After he leaves, Nikita complains, "We shouldn't even bother working so hard on this, since he's going to make us fail, no matter what we do!"

The others continue to work on the project. Giulia offers to prepare the presentation slides, if the others send her their notes. Shantel arranges for everyone come to her apartment the day before the presentation to coordinate the different parts and rehearse. Ahmad does not show up, in spite of the fact that Shantel has tried to contact him many times.

On the day of the presentation, Ahmad presents material that the team members have never heard before, and Nikita does not show up, texting Shantel that she is sick.

PRESENTATION SKILLS

Developing strong public speaking skills is one of the most important things you can do to improve your career. In the Essential Skills Profiles on Human Resources and Skills Development Canada's website (http://www.hrsdc.gc.ca/), oral communication is identified as one of the top three essential skills for nurses, paramedics, pharmacists, funeral directors, and occupational therapists.

PREPARING AND DELIVERING AN EFFECTIVE PRESENTATION

1. Identify the needs of your audience.

The purpose of your presentation is to deliver information to your audience; therefore, you need to determine exactly what they need to know. Consider how informed your audience is about the subject. Are they experts in the field, or are they members of the general public? How will you adapt your material to suit your audience?

2. Organize your information logically.

Prepare for your presentation the same way that you would prepare for writing an essay. Read up on your topic, gather your information, and organize information into a logical structure, with an introduction (including a thesis statement), a body (organized around a series of main points), and a conclusion.

3. Grab your audience's attention.

Start with a question, anecdote, quotation, or statistic. For example, you might begin a presentation on obesity like this: "Does anyone know what percentage of Canadians over the age of 18 identify themselves as obese?" The answer? 52.5%.

4. Do not read from your notes.

Avoid writing out a script for your presentation. Prepare a series of index cards with key words and main points, and practise the presentation enough that these prompts will serve as reminders of what you want to say.

5. Be aware of body language and eye contact.

Stand confidently at the front of the room, facing your audience, and use firm, authoritative hand gestures. Don't be afraid to move about. A good tip for achieving natural eye contact with your audience is to look at one person while delivering one point, and then shift your focus to another person for the next point. Try imagining that you are having a conversation with each person. Choose people at random, rather than moving mechanically across each row.

6. Use technology wisely.

Audiovisual aids can enhance a presentation, but they can also add complications and distractions. To avoid technical difficulties, ensure that all necessary equipment is set up and working properly before your presentation. If you are showing a film clip, have it cued up beforehand, and make sure that it will play. Always have a backup plan: print your slides to use as handouts, or be prepared to write on the board or on flipchart paper. When using presentation software such as PowerPoint, be careful not to distract from the content of your presentation by using too many animations, too many colours, or too much text. Keep the slides as simple as possible.

© StockLite / Shutterstock

OVERCOMING PRESENTATION ANXIETY

An infamous statistic from 1977's *Book of Lists* identifies "speaking in public" as Americans' number one fear, while death is listed at number six. While this may not be accurate, it is undeniable that the thought of addressing an audience—small or large—causes most of us to come down with a case of sweaty palms, upset stomach, and knocking knees. In fact, even Warren Buffett, the billionaire investor and philanthropist, was terrified of public speaking, but knew that he needed to overcome his fear in order to be successful.

Here are some tips for controlling your nervousness:

1. Focus on the message.

Remember that the purpose of a presentation is to deliver information to an audience. Think about the importance of the message that you need to deliver, rather than obsessing about your performance. Shifting the focus away from yourself may help to calm your nerves.

2. Practise, practise, practise.

It seems to go against logic, but the more you practise your presentation, the more natural you will seem. Don't try to memorize your talk, but do practise it as often as possible. It's especially helpful to practise in front of friends and family, to gain their feedback. You might also try filming your presentation and watching it, to catch any verbal tics (such as "ummm," "like," and "y'know"), physical habits (hair flipping, toe tapping, finger wagging), or other areas for improvement. If watching yourself on video makes you self-conscious, just remember that you are your own worst critic; others will be far more forgiving of you, and may not even notice things that make you cringe.

3. Use positive self-talk.

We're all familiar with that voice inside our head—the one that tells us that we're bound to fail, that we're not smart enough, good looking enough, or charming enough to convince people of something. That voice is wrong. Replace it with positive messages: "I spent a lot of time researching this topic and I know more about it than anyone in this room." "I have the experience to answer any questions that the audience might ask." "I have a good sense of humour, and I can use it to put the audience at ease and smooth out any bumpy patches." It's amazing how much positive self-talk can affect your confidence, and in turn your performance.

4. Learn breathing and relaxation exercises.

When we feel nervous or threatened, our bodies automatically respond by going into what is known as the fight-or-flight response. Your heart beat increases, your blood pressure rises, and your breathing becomes faster and shallower. While this state may save your life if you are in physical danger, it is not a useful response when the perceived threat is not a masked stranger, but rather a presentation in front of a group. There is a strong connection between your physical state and your mental state, so if you can calm your body, then your mind will be clearer and more focused. The best way to do this is through taking slow, deep breaths. Breathe in slowly, through your nose, for five counts, and then release the breath, through your mouth, for ten counts. Can you feel yourself becoming calmer? For more breathing and relaxation tips, see the links at the end of this chapter.

5. Fake confidence—no one will know the difference!

It's surprising how many professional public speakers confess to being almost paralyzed by nervousness before giving a presentation; yet they stride onto the stage, performing confidence, and the audience never knows how nervous they were. A side benefit of pretending to be confident is that, over the course of your presentation, it stops being a pretense, and you actually *become* more confident. One of the authors knows an accomplished lawyer who, even after many years of success, still throws up before every court appearance. Yet he strides into the courtroom, faking the confidence that he doesn't feel, and eventually he feels more confident. Everyone in the courtroom sees a confident, successful lawyer, arguing his case.

What is your biggest fear about speaking in public? (For example, it might be forgetting what you wanted to say, and standing at the front of the room with your mind a complete blank.) Write it down. Now, underneath your answer, write down what you think would happen if your biggest fear came true. What would you do in that situation? Would it really be that bad, or is it something that you could overcome quite easily?

CHARACTERISTICS OF EFFECTIVE PRESENTATIONS

The information you are presenting should be CLEAR. If possible, practise in front of a friend or family member who is unfamiliar with the topic, and ask them questions to make sure that they understand the information you have presented.

Present the material in as OBJECTIVE a manner as possible. Unless you have been specifically asked to do so, do not present your personal opinion on a topic.

Be CONCISE, and avoid rambling on during your presentation. For each point, try to limit yourself to one example. We recommend videotaping yourself practising your presentation, taking note of the wordy or confusing segments, and then eliminating them from your notes.

Ensure that your information is ORGANIZED in a logical manner. Follow the same structure that you would for a written paper: introduction; a series of main points; conclusion.

Check your facts to ensure that you are providing ACCURATE information. Remember that the purpose of your presentation is to inform your audience about your subject; therefore, it is important that you are not giving misinformation.

Proofread any slides and/or handouts carefully, to ensure that you are using CORRECT spelling and grammar. Errors are unprofessional and will damage your credibility, causing your audience to doubt you.

To ensure that your presentation is AUDIENCE-APPROPRIATE, ask yourself the following questions: "Who is my audience?" "What do they already know about the subject?" "What do they need to know about the subject?" Then, tailor your material to your audience.

While your first impulse while presenting may be to get it over with, make sure that your presentation is THOROUGH. Don't skip over important material, even if it seems obvious to you. Remember that your audience doesn't know as much about the subject as you do. Ask yourself if you are giving them all the information they need.

CHAPTER LINKS FOR FURTHER EXPLORATION

- **Skip Downing's On Course® website (http://www.oncourseworkshop.com/ Student%20Success%20Strategies.htm)**

Skip Downing's On Course® website contains many resources for students, including exercises on teamwork, which are listed under "Interdependence."

- **Toastmasters International (http://www.toastmasters.org)**

Toastmasters International is a world leader in communication and leadership development. The Toastmasters website provides tips and techniques for public speaking, including how to overcome fear and anxiety.

- **Public Speaking International (http://www.publicspeakinginternational.com)**

This site offers advice on all aspects of public speaking, from eliminating nervousness to connecting with your audience.

- **Shakeshaft, Jordan. (2012, October 8). "6 breathing exercises to relax in 10 minutes or less."** *Time.* **Retrieved from http://healthland.time. com/2012/10/08/6-breathing-exercises-to-relax-in-10-minutes-or-less**

This article provides some useful breathing exercises to help you relax before your presentation.

- **Canadian Health Services Research Foundation. (2006).** *Teamwork in healthcare: Promoting effective teamwork in healthcare in Canada.* **Ottawa: Canadian Health Services Research Foundation. Retrieved from http://www.cfhi-fcass.ca/Migrated/PDF/teamwork-synthesis-report_e.pdf**

This research report examines the characteristics of an effective healthcare team and explores the extent to which teamwork has been implemented in healthcare settings in Canada.

CREATIVE CONNECTIONS: HEALTH DISCUSSIONS AND CONTROVERSIES

At the end of this chapter, you should be able to

- think critically about issues related to illness, aging, disability, death, and disease
- express your opinions on a variety of health issues thoughtfully, confidently, and diplomatically
- engage in meaningful discussions related to health and health care
- recognize the importance of the reflective process in health care and understand how analysis and discussion of fiction can enhance that process
- format APA reference citations correctly by following model samples

INTRODUCTION

The information in the previous chapters focused mainly on helping you meet the technical requirements of your health science certificate, diploma, or degree, and equipping you for the formalities of the workplace. To be successful, a health care worker requires more than technical knowledge, however. In working with individuals in very vulnerable situations, you must also be prepared to exercise traits of patience, tolerance, compassion, understanding, and empathy. In this last chapter, you will explore and reflect upon your capacity for these traits in a unique, interesting, and thought-provoking way: through the analysis of poetry, short stories, and film.

Note: While the APA style of documentation is not used in the creative arts, the following short story, poetry, and film citations have been presented in APA style in order to model correct form.

The arts have a mesmerizing power. A story, poem, or film often seduces us because we empathize and can relate to its contents in meaningful ways. Art is about our lives and, as such, it proves the perfect medium through which to reflect on health-related themes like aging, disability, illness, disease, and death. Reflecting on such issues is an important process for the health care provider who finds him- or herself in the centre of an emotionally charged environment filled with grief, apathy, conflict, and pain. As a professional, you must navigate this complex emotional world with success, dignity, and grace.

Reflection allows health care practitioners to better address the unique needs of their clients while simultaneously managing the emotional impact of caring for others on a daily basis. Reflective practice, in the allied health fields, involves critical reflection on and analysis of the events that occur in the workplace with the understanding that such awareness is a requisite step towards providing high quality care that is effective, ethical, and compassionate.

Even though most of the characters you will encounter in this chapter are fictitious, their struggles in the areas of illness, isolation, aging, relationships, and health care reflect real-world conflicts and concerns, and may be similar to situations you will encounter in your career as a health professional.

By reading and thinking about the story, poetry, and film selections that follow, you will, hopefully, gain deeper insight and understanding into the complexities of the human condition, a necessary and important step for anyone interested in the health care field.

As you explore the stories, poems, and films herein, you will have much to contemplate long after you leave the classroom.

I remember reading a story by Vincent Lam called "Night Flight" in one of my communication classes when I was studying to be a paramedic. It was about a helicopter medic who was off to save a dying man in Guatemala. The story was amazing; it seemed so real. As I read the story, I really felt the stresses and the fast pace of the medic's lifestyle. Once I read that story, I knew that I was in the right field. I've even gone on to read other books by Lam, and they continue to give me insights into my work, now that I'm a practising paramedic. Stories educate and inspire me in a way that boring textbooks just can't.

—Paramedic graduate, Humber College

Imagine a day of work in your chosen health profession. Write your thoughts in the form of a story. You may use the first-person narrator (I) or create a third-person (he, she) identity. Walk your reader through the joys and challenges of such a day.

STORIES TO ANALYZE AND DISCUSS

The following two stories, Linda Svendsen's "White Shoulders" (1992) and Vincent Lam's "Take All of Murphy" (2005), provide useful and provocative insights into the world of illness and health care. Exploring diverse themes like illness, suicide, grief, and conflicts between the personal and professional, both stories are rich in material to discuss and debate. In "White Shoulders," a family member's diagnosis of cancer wreaks further devastation on an already dysfunctional family. In "Take All of Murphy," three medical students are confronted with some surprising personal and ethical challenges as they dissect a cadaver in their anatomy course. Read each story carefully and then work in small groups to discuss the questions that follow each reading.

"WHITE SHOULDERS," by Linda Svendsen

My oldest sister's name is Irene de Haan and she has never hurt anybody. She lives with cancer, in remission, and she has stayed married to the same undemonstrative Belgian Canadian, a brake specialist, going on thirty years. In the family's crumbling domestic empire, Irene and Peter's union has been, quietly, and despite tragedy, what our mother calls the lone success.

Back in the late summer of 1984, before Irene was admitted into hospital for removal of her left breast, I flew home from New York to Vancouver to be with her. We hadn't seen each other for four years, and since I didn't start teaching ESL night classes until mid-September, I was free, at loose ends, unlike the rest of her family. Over the past months, Peter had used up vacation and personal days shuttling her to numerous tests, but finally had to get back to work. He still had a mortgage. Their only child, Jill, who'd just turned seventeen, was entering her last year of high school. Until junior high, she'd been one of those unnaturally well-rounded kids—taking classes in the high dive, water ballet, drawing, and drama, and boy-hunting in the mall on Saturdays with a posse of dizzy friends. Then, Irene said, overnight she became unathletic, withdrawn, and bookish: an academic drone. At any rate, for Jill and Pete's sake, Irene didn't intend to allow her illness to interfere with their life. She wanted everything to proceed as normally as possible. As who wouldn't.

In a way, and this will sound callous, the timing had worked out. Earlier that summer, my ex-husband had been offered a temporary teaching position across the country, and after a long dinner at our old Szechuan dive, I'd agreed to temporarily revise our custody arrangement. With his newfound bounty, Bill would rent a California town house for nine months and royally support the kids. "Dine and Disney," he'd said.

I'd blessed this, but then missed them. I found myself dead asleep in the middle of the day in Jane's lower bunk, or tuning in late afternoon to my six-year-old son's, and Bill's, obsession, *People's Court*. My arms ached when I saw other women holding sticky hands, pulling frenzied children along behind them in the August dog days.

So I flew west. To be a mother again, I'd jokingly told Irene over the phone. To serve that very need.

Peter was late meeting me at the airport. We gave each other a minimal hug, and then he shouldered my bags and walked ahead out into the rain. The Datsun was double-parked, hazards flashing, with a homemade sign taped on the rear window that said STUD. DRIVER. "Jill," he said, loading the trunk. "Irene's been teaching her so she can pick up the groceries. Help out for a change." I got in, he turned on easy-listening, and we headed north towards the grey mountains.

Irene had been in love with him since I was a child; he'd been orphaned in Belgium during World War II, which moved both Irene and our mother. He'd also reminded us of Emile, the Frenchman in *South Pacific*, because he was greying, autocratic, and seemed misunderstood. But the European charm had gradually worn thin; over the years, I'd been startled by Peter's racism and petty tyranny. I'd often wished that the young Irene had been fondled off her two feet by a breadwinner more tender, more local. Nobody else in the family agreed and Mum even hinted that I'd become bitter since the demise of my own marriage.

"So how is she?" I finally asked Peter.

"She's got a cold," he said, "worrying herself sick. And other than that, it's hard to say." His tone was markedly guarded. He said prospects were poor; the lump was large and she had the fast-growing, speedy sort of cancer. "But she thinks the Paki quack will get it when he cuts," he said.

I sat with that. "And how's Jill?"

"Grouchy," he said. "Bitchy." This gave me pause, and it seemed to have the same effect on him.

We pulled into the garage of the brick house they'd lived in since Jill's birth, and he waved me on while he handled the luggage. The house seemed smaller now, tucked under tall Douglas firs and fringed with baskets of acutely pink geraniums and baby's breath. The back door was open, so I walked in; the master bedroom door was ajar, but I knocked first. She wasn't there. Jill called, "Aunt Adele?" and I headed back down the hall to the guestroom, and stuck my head in.

A wan version of my sister rested on a water bed in the dark. When I plunked down I made a tiny wave. Irene almost smiled. She was thin as a fine chain; in my embrace, her flesh barely did the favour of keeping her bones company. Her blondish hair was quite short, and she looked ordinary, like a middle-aged matron who probably worked at a bank and kept a no-fail punch recipe filed away. I had to hold her, barely, close again. Behind us, the closet was full of her conservative garments—flannel, floral—and I understood that this was her room now. She slept here alone. She didn't frolic with Peter any more, have sex.

"Don't cling," Irene said slowly, but with her old warmth. "Don't get melo-dramatic. I'm not dying. It's just a cold."

"Aunt Adele," Jill said.

I turned around; I'd forgotten my niece was even there, and she was sitting right on the bed, wedged against a bolster. We kissed hello with loud smooch effects—our ritual—and while she kept a hand on Irene's shoulder, she stuttered answers to my questions about school and her summer. Irene kept an eye on a mute TV—the U.S. Open—although she didn't have much interest in tennis; I sensed, really, that she didn't have any extra energy available for banter. This was conservation, not rudeness.

Jill looked different. In fact, the change in her appearance and demeanour exceeded the ordinary drama of puberty; she seemed to be another girl—sly, unsure, and unable to look in the eye. She wore silver wire glasses, no makeup, jeans with an oversize kelly-green sweatshirt, and many extra pounds. Her soft strawcoloured hair was pulled back with a swan barrette, the swan's eye downcast. When she passed Irene a glass of water and a pill, Irene managed to swallow, then passed it back, and Jill drank, too. To me, it seemed she took great care, twisting the glass in her hand, to sip from the very spot her mother's lips had touched.

Peter came in, sat down on Jill's side of the bed, and stretched both arms around to raise the back of his shirt. He bared red, hairless skin, and said, "Scratch."

"But I'm watching tennis," Jill said softly.

"But you're my daughter," he said. "And I have an itch."

Peter looked at Irene and she gave Jill a sharp nudge. "Do your poor dad," she said. "You don't even have to get up."

"But aren't I watching something?" Jill said. She glanced around, searching for an ally.

"*Vrouw*," Peter spoke up. "This girl, she doesn't do anything except mope, eat, mope, eat."

Jill's shoulders sagged slightly, as if all air had suddenly abandoned her body, and then she slowly got up. "I'll see you after, Aunt Adele," she whispered, and I said, "Yes, sure," and then she walked out.

Irene looked dismally at Peter; he made a perverse sort of face—skewing his lips south. Then she reached over and started to scratch his bare back. It was an effort. "Be patient with her, Peter," she said. "She's worried about the surgery."

"She's worried you won't be around to wait on her," Peter said, then instructed, "Go a little higher." Irene's fingers crept obediently up. "Tell Adele what Jill said."

Irene shook her head. "I don't remember."

Peter turned to me. "When Irene told her about the cancer, she said, 'Don't die on me, Mum, or I'll kill you.' And she said this so serious. Can you imagine?" Peter laughed uninhibitedly, and then Irene joined in, too, although her quiet accompaniment was forced. There wasn't any recollected pleasure in her eyes at all; rather, it seemed as if she didn't want Peter to laugh alone, to appear as odd as he did. "Don't die or I'll kill you," Peter said.

*****

Irene had always been private about her marriage. If there were disagreements with Peter, and there had been—I'd once dropped in unannounced and witnessed a string of Christmas lights whip against the fireplace and shatter—they were never rebroadcast to the rest of the family; if she was ever discouraged or lonely, she didn't confide in anyone, unless she kept a journal or spoke to her God. She had never said a word against the man.

The night before Irene's surgery, after many earnest wishes and ugly flowers had been delivered, she asked me to stay late with her at Lion's Gate Hospital. The room had emptied. Peter had absconded with Jill—and she'd gone reluctantly, asking to stay until I left—and our mother, who'd been so nervous and sad that an intern had fed her Valium from his pocket. "Why is this happening to her?" Mum said to him. "To my only happy child."

Irene, leashed to an IV, raised herself to the edge of the bed and looked out at the parking lot and that kind Pacific twilight. "That Jill," Irene said. She allowed her head to fall, arms crossed in front of her. "She should lift a finger for her father."

"Well," I said, watching my step, aware she needed peace, "Peter's not exactly the most easygoing."

"No," she said weakly.

We sat for a long time, Irene in her white gown, me beside her in my orange-and-avocado track suit, until I began to think I'd been too tough on Peter and had distressed her. Then she spoke. "Sometimes I wish I'd learned more Dutch," she said neutrally. "When I met Peter, we married not speaking the same language, really. And that made a difference."

She didn't expect a comment—she raised her head and stared out the half-open window—but I was too shocked to respond anyway. I'd never heard her remotely suggest that her and Peter's marriage had been less than a living storybook. "You don't like him, do you?" she said. "You don't care for his Belgian manner."

I didn't answer; it didn't need to be said aloud. I turned away. "I'm probably not the woman who can best judge these things," I said.

Out in the hall, a female patient talked on the phone. Irene and I both listened. "I left it in the top drawer," she said wearily. "No. The *bedroom*." There was a pause. "The desk in the hall, try that." Another pause. "Then ask Susan where she put it, because I'm tired of this and I need it." I turned as she hung the phone up and saw her check to see if money had tumbled back. The hospital was quiet again. Irene did not move, but she was shaking; I found it difficult to watch this and reached out and took her hand.

"What is it?" I said. "Irene."

She told me she was scared. Not for herself, but for Peter. That when she had first explained to him about the cancer, he hadn't spoken to her for three weeks. Or touched her. Or kissed her. He'd slept in the guestroom, until she'd offered to move there. And he'd been after Jill to butter his toast, change the sheets, iron his pants. Irene had speculated about this, she said, until she'd realized he was acting this way because of what had happened to him when he was little. In Belgium. Bruges, the war. He had only confided in her once. He'd said all the women he'd ever loved had left him. His mother killed, his sister. "And now me," Irene said. "The big C which leads to the big D. If I move on, I leave two children. And I've told Jill they have to stick together."

I got off the bed. "But Irene," I said, "she's not on earth to please her father. Who can be unreasonable. In my opinion."

By this time, a medical team was touring the room. The junior member paused by Irene and said, "Give me your vein."

"In a minute," she said to him, "please," and he left. There were dark areas, the colour of new bruises, under her eyes. "I want you to promise me something."

"Yes."

"If I die," she said, "and I'm not going to, but if I do, I don't want Jill to live with you in New York. Because that's what she wants to do. I want her to stay with Peter. Even if she runs to you, send her back."

"I can't promise that," I said. "Because you're not going to go anywhere."

She looked at me. Pale, fragile. She was my oldest sister, who'd always been zealous about the silver lining in that cloud; and now it seemed she might be dying, in her forties—too soon—and she needed to believe I could relieve her of this burden. So I nodded, *Yes.*

***

When I got back, by cab, to Irene and Peter's that night, the house was dark. I groped up the back steps, ascending through a hovering scent of honeysuckle, stepped inside, and turned on the kitchen light. The TV was going—some ultra-loud camera commercial—in the living room. Nobody was watching. "Jill?" I said. "Peter?"

I wandered down the long hall, snapping on switches: Irene's sickroom, the upstairs bathroom, the master bedroom, Peter's domain. I did a double-take; he was there. Naked, lying on top of the bed, his still hand holding his penis—as if to keep it warm and safe—the head shining. The blades of the ceiling fan cut in slow circles above him. His eyes were vague and didn't turn my way; he was staring up. "Oh sorry," I whispered, "God, sorry," and flicked the light off again.

I headed back to the living room and sat, for a few seconds. When I'd collected myself, I went to find Jill. She wasn't in her downstairs room, which seemed typically adolescent in decor—Boy George poster, socks multiplying in a corner—until I spotted a quote from Rilke, in careful purple handwriting, taped for her long mirror: "Beauty is only the first touch of terror we can still bear."

I finally spotted the light under the basement bathroom door.

"Jill," I said. "It's me."

"I'm in the bathroom," she said.

"I know," I said. "I want to talk."

She unlocked the door and let me in. She looked tense and peculiar; it looked as if she'd just thrown water on her face. She was still dressed in her clothes from the hospital—from the day before, the kelly-green sweat job—and she'd obviously been sitting on the edge of the tub, writing. There was a Papermate, a pad of yellow legal paper. The top sheet was covered with verses of tiny backward-slanting words. There was also last night's pot of Kraft Dinner on the sink. "You're all locked in," I said.

She didn't comment, and when the silence stretched on too long I said, "Homework?" and pointed to the legal pad.

"No," she said. Then she gave me a look and said, "Poem." "Oh," I said, and I was surprised. "Do you ever show them? Or it?" "No," she said. "They're not very good." She sat back down on the tub. "But maybe I'd show you, Aunt Adele."

"Good," I said. "Not that I'm a judge." I told her Irene was tucked in and that she was in a better, more positive frame of mind. More like herself. This seemed to relax Jill so much, I marched the lie a step further. "Once your mum is out of the woods," I said, "your father may lighten up." "That day will never come," she said.

"Never say never," I said. I gave her a hug—she was so much bigger than my daughter, but I embraced her the same way I had Jane since she was born: a hand and a held kiss on the top of the head.

She hugged me back. "Maybe I'll come live with you, Auntie A." "Maybe," I said, mindful of Irene's wishes. "You and everybody," and saw the disappointment on her streaked face. So I added, "Everything will be all right. Wait and see. She'll be all right."

* * *

And Irene was. They claimed they'd got it, and ten days later she came home, earlier than expected. When Peter, Jill, and I were gathered around her in the sickroom, Irene started cracking jokes about her future prosthetic fitting. "How about the Dolly Parton, hon?" she said to Peter. "Then I'd be a handful."

I was surprised to see Peter envelop her in his arm; I hadn't ever seen him offer an affectionate gesture. He told her he didn't care what size boob she bought, because breasts were for the hungry babies—not so much for the husband. "I have these," he said. "These are mine. These big white shoulders." And he rested his head against her shoulder and looked placidly at Jill; he was heavy, but Irene used her other arm to bolster herself, hold him up, and she closed her eyes in what seemed to be joy. Jill came and sat by me.

* * *

Irene took it easy the next few days; I stuck by, as did Jill, when she ventured in after school. I was shocked that there weren't more calls, or cards, or visitors except for Mum, and I realized my sister's life was actually very narrow, or extremely focused: family came first. Even Jill didn't seem to have any friends at all; the phone never rang for her.

Then Irene suddenly started to push herself—she prepared a complicated deep-fried Belgian dish; in the afternoon, she sat with Jill, in the Datsun, while Jill practiced parallel parking in front of the house and lobbied for a mother-daughter trip to lovely downtown Brooklyn for Christmas. And then, after a long nap and a little dinner, Irene insisted on attending the open house at Jill's school.

We were sitting listening to the band rehearse, a *Flashdance* medley, when I became aware of Irene's body heat—she was on my right—and asked if she might not want to head home. She was burning up. "Let me get through this," she said. Then Jill, on my other side, suddenly said in a small tight voice, "Mum." She was staring her mother's blouse, where a bright stitch of scarlet had shown up. Irene had bled through her dressing. Irene looked down. "Oh," she said. "Peter."

On the tear to the hospital, Peter said he'd sue Irene's stupid "Paki bugger" doctor. He also said he should take his stupid wife to court for loss of sex. He should get a divorce for no-nookie. For supporting a one-tit wonder. And on and on.

Irene wasn't in shape to respond; I doubt she would have anyway.

Beside me in the back seat, Jill turned to stare out the window; she was white, sitting on her hands.

I found my voice. "I don't think we need to hear this right now, Peter," I said.

"Oh, Adele," Irene said warningly. Disappointed.

He pulled over, smoothly, into a bus zone. Some of the people waiting for the bus weren't pleased. Peter turned and faced me, his finger punctuating. "This is my wife, my daughter, my Datsun." He paused. "I can say what the hell I want. And you're welcome to walk." He reached over and opened my door.

The two women at the bus shelter hurried away, correctly sensing an incident.

"I'm going with Aunt—" Jill was barely audible.

"No," said Irene. "You stay here."

I sat there, paralyzed. I wanted to get out, but didn't want to leave Irene and Jill alone with him; Irene was very ill, Jill seemed defenceless. "Look," I said to Peter, "forget I said anything. Let's just get Irene there, okay?"

He pulled the door shut, then turned front, checked me in the rearview one last time—cold, intimidating—and headed off again. Jill was crying silently. The insides of her glasses were smeared; I shifted over beside her and she linked her arm through mine tight, tight. Up front, Irene did not move.

* * *

They said it was an infection which had spread to the chest wall, requiring antibiotics and hospital admission. They were also going to perform more tests.

Peter took off with Jill, saying that they both had to get up in the morning.

Before I left Irene, she spoke to me privately, in a curtained cubicle in Emergency, and asked if I could stay at our mother's for the last few days of my visit; Irene didn't want to hurt me, but she thought it would be better, for all concerned, if I cleared out.

And then she went on; her fever was high, but she was lucid and fighting hard to stay that way. Could I keep quiet about this to our mother? And stop gushing about the East to Jill, going on about the Statue of Liberty and the view of the water from the window in the crown? And worry a little more about my own lost children and less about her daughter? And try to be more understanding of her husband, who sometimes wasn't able to exercise control over his emotions? Irene said Peter needed more love, more time; more of her, God willing. After that, she couldn't speak. And, frankly, neither could I.

I gave in to everything she asked. Jill and Peter dropped in together during the evening to see her; I visited Irene, with Mum, during the day when Peter was at work. Our conversations were banal and strained—they didn't seem to do either of us much good. After I left her one afternoon, I didn't know where I was going and ended up at my father's grave. I just sat there, on top of it, on the lap of the stone.

The day before my New York flight, I borrowed my mother's car to pick up a prescription for her at the mall. I was window-shopping my way back to the parking lot, when I saw somebody resembling my niece sitting on a bench outside a sporting goods store. At first, the girl seemed too dishevelled, too dirty-looking, actually, to be Jill, but as I approached, it became clear it was her. She wasn't doing anything. She sat there, draped in her mother's London Fog raincoat, her hands resting on her thickish thighs, clicking a barrette open, closed, open, closed. It was ten in the morning; she should have been at school. In English. For a moment, it crossed my mind that she might be on drugs: this was a relief; it would explain everything. But I didn't think she was. I was going to go over and simply say, *Yo, Jill, let's do tea*, and then I remembered my sister's frightening talk with me at the hospital and thought, *Fuck it. Butt out, Adele*, and walked the long way round. I turned my back.

* * *

One sultry Saturday morning, in late September—after I'd been back in Brooklyn for a few weeks—I was up on the roof preparing the first lessons for classes, when the super brought a handful of mail up. He'd been delivering it personally to tenants since the box had been ripped out of the entrance wall. It was the usual stuff and a thin white business envelope from Canada. From Jill. I opened it: *Dearlingest [sic] Aunt Adele, These are my only copies. Love, your only niece, Jill. P.S. I'm going to get a job and come see you at Easter.*

There were two. The poems were carefully written, each neat on their single page, with the script leaning left, as if blown by a stiff breeze. "Black Milk" was about three deaths: before her beloved husband leaves for war, a nursing mother shares a bottle of old wine with him, saved from their wedding day, and unknowingly poisons her child and then herself. Dying, she rocks her dying child in her arms, but her last conscious thought is for her husband at the front. Jill had misspelled wedding; she'd put *weeding*.

"Belgium" described a young girl ice skating across a frozen lake—Jill had been to Belgium with her parents two times—fleeing an unnamed pursuer. During each quick, desperate glide, the ice melts beneath her until, at the end, she is underwater: "In the deep cold / Face to face / Look, he comes now / My Father / My Maker." The girl wakes up; it was a bad dream. And then her earthly father appears in her bed and, "He makes night / Come again / All night," by covering her eyes with his large, heavy hand.

I read these, and read them again, and I wept. I looked out, past the steeples and the tar roofs, where I thought I saw the heat rising, toward the green of Prospect Park, and held the poems in my lap, flat under my two hands. I didn't know what to do;

I didn't know what to do right away; I thought I should wait until I knew clearly what to say and whom to say it to.

***

In late October, Mum phoned, crying, and said that Irene's cancer had not been caught by the mastectomy. Stray cells had been detected in other areas of her body. Chemotherapy was advised. Irene had switched doctors; she was seeing a naturopath. She was paying big money for an American miracle gum, among other things.

Mum also said that Jill had disappeared for thirty-two hours. Irene claimed that Jill had been upset because of a grade—a C in Phys Ed. Mum didn't believe it was really that; she thought Irene's condition was disturbing Jill, but hadn't said that to Irene.

She didn't volunteer any information about the other member of Irene's family and I did not ask.

***

In November, Bill came east for a visit and brought the children, as scheduled; he also brought a woman named Cheryl Oak. The day before Thanksgiving, the two of them were invited to a dinner party, and I took Graham and Jane, taller and both painfully shy with me, to Central Park. It was a crisp, windy night. We watched the gi-normous balloons being blown up for the Macy's parade and bought roasted chestnuts, not to eat, but to warm the palms of our hands. I walked them back to their hotel and delivered them to the quiet, intelligent person who would probably become their stepmother, and be good to them, as she'd obviously been for Bill. Later, back in Brooklyn, I was still awake—wondering how another woman had succeeded with my husband and, now, my own little ones—when Irene phoned at 3 a.m. She told me Jill was dead. "There's been an accident," she said.

A few days later, my mother and stepfather picked me up at the Vancouver airport on a warm, cloudy morning. On the way to the funeral, they tried to tell me, between them—between breakdowns—what had happened. She had died of hypothermia; the impact of hitting the water had most likely rendered her unconscious. She probably hadn't been aware of drowning, but she'd done that, too. She'd driven the Datsun to Stanley Park—she'd told Irene she was going to the library—left the key in the ignition, walked not quite to the middle of the bridge, and hoisted herself over the railing. There was one eye-witness: a guy who worked in a video store. He'd kept saying, "It was like a movie, I saw this little dumpling girl just throw herself off."

The chapel was half-empty, and the director mumbled that that was unusual when a teenager passed on. Irene had not known, and neither had Mum, where to reach Joyce, our middle sister, who was missing as usual; Ray, our older brother, gave a short eulogy. He stated that he didn't believe in any God, but Irene did, and he was glad for that this day. He also guessed that when any child takes her own life, the whole family must wonder why, and probably do that forever. The face of my sister was not to be borne. Then we all sang "The Water Is Wide," which Jill had once performed in an elementary-school talent show. She'd won Honourable Mention.

After the congregation dispersed, Peter remained on his knees, his head in his hands, while Irene approached the casket. Jill wore a pale pink dress and her other glasses, and her hair was pinned back, as usual, with a barrette—this time, a dove. Irene bent and kissed her on the mouth, on the forehead, then tugged at Jill's lace collar, adjusting it just so. It was the eternal mother's gesture, that finishing touch, before your daughter sails out the door on her big date.

I drank to excess at the reception; we all did, and needed to. Irene and I did not exchange a word; we just held each other for a long minute. From a distance, and that distance was necessary, I heard Peter talking about Belgium and memories of his childhood. On his fifth birthday, his sister, Kristin, had sent him a pencil from Paris, a new one, unsharpened, and he had used it until the lead was gone and it was so short he could barely hold it between his fingers. On the morning his mother was shot, in cold blood, he'd been dressing in the dark. The last thing she had said, to the Germans, was "Don't hurt my little boy." This was when Mum and I saw Irene go to him and take his hand. She led him down the hall to his bedroom and closed the door behind them. "Thank God," Mum said. "Thank God, they have each other. Thank God, she has him."

And for that moment, I forget about the despair that had prompted Jill to do what she did, and my own responsibility and silence, because I was alive and full of needs, sickness, and dreams myself. I thought, *No, I will never tell my sister what I suspect, because life is short and very hard*, and I thought, *Yes, a bad marriage is better than none*, and I thought, *Adele, let the sun go down on your anger, because it will not bring her back*, and I turned to my mother. "Yes," I said. "Thank God."

Source: From "White shoulders" reprinted from MARINE LIFE by Linda Svendsen. Copyright © 1982 by Linda Svendsen. Published by HarperCollins Publishers, Ltd. Reprinted by permission of the Author and Robin Straus Agency, Inc., New York.

Model APA citation

Svendsen, L. (1995). White shoulders. In M. Atwood & R. Weaver (Eds.), *The Oxford book of Canadian short stories in English* (pp. 413–422). Toronto, Canada: Oxford University Press. (Original work published 1992)

Discussion Questions:

1. According to Adele, the narrator of the story and Irene's sister, how has cancer physically affected Irene?

2. How does Irene's cancer appear to affect Jill?

3. How does Irene's cancer appear to affect Peter?

4. What do you think is meant by Jill's statement when she is first told about her mother's cancer: "Don't die on me, Mum, or I'll kill you"?

5. What does Irene appear to be most concerned about throughout her illness?

6. Do Peter's various expressions of anger toward Irene surprise you? Why or why not?

7. What is ironic about the following line from the story: "Irene said Peter needed more love, more time; more of her, God willing."

8. What do Jill's poems suggest about her state of mind at the time of her suicide?

9. In the last paragraph of the story, Adele states, "No. I will never tell my sister what I suspect...." What exactly is it that Adele suspects?

10. Do you think Svendsen's portrayal of how illness can damage a family is realistic? Why or why not?

11. Have you, or someone you are close to, ever been affected by a serious illness? How did you and/or your loved one cope?

12. What advice or support would you offer a family trying to cope with a difficult situation like the one in "White Shoulders"?

"TAKE ALL OF MURPHY," by Vincent Lam

The three students stood beside the wrapped body lying on the metal table. They all wore clean new laboratory coats, which still had creases down the arms and over the breast pockets from being folded and stacked in a box. These white coats were the same size, even though the wearers were of varying build. All three medical students were size medium, but differently framed. Ming had her cuffs rolled up twice.

They had come in from the hot, early afternoon of an autumn day, a remnant of summer. They had entered the basement by an unmarked inner staircase, and then approached the lab through a plain, combination-locked door. There were fourteen dissection rooms, eight tables per room, three students assigned per table, checking the tags to find their cadavers, whispering and shuffling like white-coated ghosts in the basement anatomy lab. No windows. Instead, a dry fluorescent light flattened every surface.

"You want to go first?" said Ming.

"I don't mind," said Sri.

"Me neither," said Chen, holding the blade hesitantly between his thumb, and the second and third fingers.

"Well to me, it doesn't matter," said Ming. "What about you?" she asked, turning to Sri. When he paused, she said, "If it's a problem for you I'll start the cutting."

To Sri, Ming seemed both overly eager and fearful regarding the task, and Sri did not want their dissection to begin with this mix of emotions. Sri felt only the single emotion of fear, which he felt was a better way to begin this undertaking, and so he said,

"I'll start." He gripped his blade handle firmly.

"Not if you don't want to," said Chen, seeing Sri's discomfort. "I can."

"I'll start." Sri shifted closer.

* * *

That morning, they had been briefed in the lecture theatre by Dean Cortina, "A few of you might be upset initially. You may temporarily excuse yourselves if necessary. In any case, I would rather you be a bit emotional than, shall we say, overly cavalier. Keep in mind that distasteful incidents regarding cadavers have, in the past, resulted in expulsion."

She reminded them that there was to be no eating or drinking in the dissection rooms, although snacks could be consumed in the anatomy museum so long as it was kept tidy.

* * *

"I think it's easier if you hold it like a pen," said Ming. When Sri said nothing, she said, "All I'm saying it that if you hold it like a ... Well, never mind, suit yourself of course, it's only that-"

"Just let me do it," said Sri. "Let me stand here." He moved to stand where Ming was, without waiting for her to move. She shifted, avoiding collision. Ming and Chen were quiet.

Sri began to cut the cotton, a stringy damp net, discoloured yellow in its folds. It smelled tough. First he cut down like when you lean with the first finger on a boned meat. This dented it, but the fabric was swelling inwards instead of giving. He turned the scalpel upwards, and lifted the edge of the fabric to slip the blade beneath the fabric. He sawed back and forth, and the threads twisted when severed.

"What about scissors?" whispered Chen.

Dr. Harrison, their anatomy demonstrator, appeared at their table, congratulated them upon entering the study of medicine, and said, "This fine cadaver is your first patient. Dignity and decorum are crucial. You must be mindful of this gift you are given, and treat your patient nobly." He paused. "Nobility. You may give him ... or her?"

Harrison checked the tag. "Ah, him, a name if you like. Or not. That's up to you. No frivolous names. Questions? No? Very well. Continue, then." All of this, he managed to say with his hands crossed neatly in front of himself, and then he was at the next table, nodding seriously.

The fabric now open, Ming took scissors and cut it wider in a quick, impatient motion, spreading the fabric up to the neck and then down to the navel. The damp skin of the cadaver's chest was a shocking beige within the yellowed fabric that had been cut apart.

"There," said Ming.

"Are you going to do it?" said Sri, not offering the scalpel. He hadn't moved, and she had leaned across him to open the swath of cloth.

"I was just trying to help, you know, get things going."

"I already said I'll do it."

"As you prefer."

Sri now held the scalpel like a pen. He looked at the manual. The manual was very particular, and Sri wanted to follow it with clarity. At the top of the sternum the incision should begin, extending downwards to the xiphoid. *A central incision*, it read. Ming opened the fabric, pulled it to either side, the nipples purple on the rubber-cold skin. Still not moving, Sri held the scalpel like a pen, stared at the manual's exact instructions. There was a dotted line drawn from the top of the sternum in the illustration, an arrow pointed towards the navel but stopping short of it. Sri straightened the veil, covered the nipples. He gripped the scalpel hard, like a dull pencil.

"Right down the middle," said Ming. "Like a zipper. But if you're going to take forever—"

Sri grabbed the scalpel handle like a stick, and buried the short, triangular blade in the midline of the chest. Flesh gripped the blade, and through the handle Sri felt its texture—thick and chalky. Steel scraping on sternum. Sri thought of a beach—of writing with a stick in hard sand thrown halfway up from the tide, with the water not far away. Through his knuckles, Sri felt fibres tearing. The cadaver's flesh pulled hard at him now. Halfway there. It ripped at Sri, to cut this skin. He tore it, forced his way through. He pulled open the cotton shroud. This old, wrung-out chest with small lopsided man-breasts. Above the left nipple were four tattoo hearts in purple, the shape of the designs twisted by the skin's movement through its years. A clean jagged tear through the centre—the sternum white beneath. Sri was amazed by the pale ivory of a man's bone.

The three of them stood erect at the shining cold table. The man now lay slightly unwrapped. The cloths wound around themselves up and over his neck, then tenderly wrapped the face. They had been told the heads would all be shaved. The table was indented, and the indentation traced down to a hole between the feet. The hole opened into a spout over a bucket so fluids could escape as they ran down the table. On the steel was the man-form in soaked cloth. His chest was gashed now. The chest was not shaved but was thick with cold hair. Hair parted in one crooked stabbing cut which peeled open the front.

"Good job, Sri," said Chen.

"Feels funny."

"I guess it's my turn."

There were eight dissection tables in the room, and at some tables a person was hunched over a cadaver. Whispers shuddered up from the floor, as the familiar touch of skin became distorted. One hushed voice: *Haven't we all seen bodies before?* At another, one held the cloth up and the other two cut at it. All of the students wore new lab coats, which they had been told they would need to discard once the dissection was done.

* * *

One day when Chen was in Dean Cortina's office to discuss student loans, she said to him, "I remember my dissection group. Oh, what year, I don't want to tell you. I remember some comments that were made—regarding dissection material. You see, in my time it was all people from the jails or found dead in fights or ditches. No identification and so forth. What you would call bad people. Yours are different, all volunteers. Elderly, upstanding citizens mostly. Ours were young people with fast lifestyles. Virile, some might say. Although I guess it's really no different once they're cadavers.

"Anyhow. I remember some guy saying, 'Wow look at this one, what a broad.' I didn't like that, you know, I didn't think it was right. On the other hand, I remember we dissected a big man. Muscular, built, and someone called him an ox … it was to say what a powerful man, a big strong man. So they called him an 'ox.' Vernacular to be sure, but it was out of respect and to say he must have been impressive. I thought that was alright. I didn't like someone saying 'What a broad,' though. What was he looking at? That sort of sexual appeal was not the right way to think. I spoke up, oh certainly I did, I said to this guy who was laughing, 'You wouldn't like a man calling your sister a broad.' He was angry. He was pissed off and he said, 'My sister is alive so shut up.'"

Dean Cortina laughed. "So I said, 'It's not cool to call your sister a broad because she's alive?' Boy, he was upset."

Chen didn't know quite how to respond, so he agreed in a polite and very general way, and left without resolving the issue of his student loan.

* * *

On the day the ribs were cut to get at the organs, the room shrieked with handheld rotary saws. Bone dust—it was in your hair, on your lips afterwards.

"Smells like barbeque," shouted Ming.

Sri leaned off the saw, held it, still buzzing, in front of him, and regarded Ming is if amazed at her. As if about to speak. Instead, he diverted his eyes from her and said, "Where's the manual?"

Chen walked out quickly, his hand over his mouth, almost running. When he came back he was red and wet in the face, his hair pushed back and damp. "I'm fine. Are you finished cutting?"

The chest opened to show the heart's chambers, where the great vessels now lay at rest. These sinuous vessels coursed to the lungs, and splayed into the organs and limbs. The lungs were fringed with the gritty black of tobacco.

"Aren't there people who fill their dead with stones," murmured Chen, "and sink them to the bottom of the sea?"

"You're thinking of concrete boots. Gangsters did that." Ming didn't look up as she peeled away a strip of fat.

"No, after they die naturally. As a burial ceremony. They take out the heart and lungs and fill this," he patted the inside wall of the chest, "with stones so the body sinks."

"What do they do with the organs?" asked Ming.

"I can't remember that part. Who are they?" He turned to Sri.

Ming turned to Sri, "Do your people do that?"

"We burn them."

"Must smell," said Ming.

"What do you think?"

"I guess it smells. Like cutting bone. Like—", she laughed, "forget it."

Sri said little for the rest of the lab, and his quietness spilled uncomfortably to the other two, so that all three of them worked in a thick silence for the rest of the day. Cutting through layers, spreading tissue, saying only what was necessary.

Sri changed all his clothing at the lab. Many people kept a shirt or coveralls in their lockers for dissection, but Sri changed everything—his underwear, his socks, in the men's room. Always in a stall, preferably with no one else in the washroom. That day, he heard footsteps come into the bathroom a moment after he had taken off his shirt. He kept still, a reflex. The footsteps were not followed by running water, or the hissing of urine on porcelain. The footsteps waited,

"Uh—Sri? Is that you, Sri?" It was Chen.

A pause. "Yeah."

"You're cool, right?"

"Yeah."

"Great. I'm glad. Ming's got a tough exterior. Right? All bluff, you can see that."

"I said I'm cool."

"I'll see you, then."

No further footsteps.

Sri crossed his arms, his naked chest prickling in the concrete block basement.

"It's fine, Chen. Thanks for asking."

"Right. See you."

Footsteps, the squeaky door.

* * *

When they first started the dissections, there were bright mornings to come in from, and warm afternoons to go out to after the day's work. As the weeks passed, they entered the basement on cooler mornings with a hesitant light, and departed into a fading golden afternoon. The leaves swelled with colour until they became too heavy with the intensity of reds and oranges, and fell to the ground. Each day, more human anatomy was exposed, more of the organs lifted out of their shy hiding places into their first glimpse of light. It was as if the actual daytime no longer existed. Night was just ending as the students arrived in the morning, just beginning as they left. The daytime of sun had been replaced by the fluorescent bathed, whitewashed concrete daylight of the basement, as the inverted parts of bodies were given their belated and temporary glimpses of light.

Sri proposed they name their cadaver "Murphy." A dignified, but comfortable name, he argued. Ming refused to use any name. Chen took neither side, suggested that each do as they please. Sri referred to "Murphy's aorta, Murphy's kidneys." Ming made a point of saying "the cadaver's aorta, the cadaver's kidneys."

Beneath the shield of diaphragm, the liver and spleen were wet and heavy. There was a stickiness to the smell where the formalin had seeped into hepatocytes and gelled the lobes of liver into a single pungent mass.

* * *

One day the bowel tore. A line of shit squirted onto Ming's coat. It smelled like formalin, an acidic sweetness, and another smell. She wiped it off, leaving a mark, finished tracing the mesenteric circulation, and laughed when she threw the coat into the garbage. "I wanted a new coat, anyhow," she said. The cuffs of her fresh coat were again too long, and soaked up fluids until she rolled them back. It became easier to dissect, as over the days the cadaver was more fragmented and the pieces more separated from one another. There was less to pry apart—it was more detail work now.

They unwrapped the arm from the wrist upwards. The hand was separately wrapped. Ming held up the arm, holding the hand like a victory grasp. Along the flat back of the forearm was a lightning bolt tattoo, once straight lines—now soft arcs. Each branch of the lightning underlined a word. One *Golden*, the other *Flash*. Chen rolled back the moist, yellow gauze. Above the elbow was a ring of small figures, crosses? No, airplanes. In addition to the thumbprint-sized fuselage and wings, there were the remnants of little propellers, now faded into age spots and the creases of oldness. Above the airplanes in official type was tattooed *RCAF—17th Squadron*. Above this, there was a Spitfire with an open shark's jaw. The tail of the spitfire was ajar from a thick scar across the fuselage that had been sewn shut dirty, long ago. The little ring of airplanes stood wing to wing on the front above the elbow, and then a gap in the inside of the arm.

"Go killer," said Ming triumphantly. Then when they looked at her, "All those planes. He must have shot them down. You'll have to call him Lieutenant Murphy."

"A pilot?" said Chen.

"There's some planes missing," said Ming. "He didn't get enough to go all the way around."

Sri touched the tattooed arm. "I guess the war ended."

"It's good they started the tattoos from the outside," said Ming.

Chen bunched up the gauze and snipped it. He continued to unroll, revealing a rich and delicate crucifix within a heart, large over the hump of shoulder. In gothic letters under the crucifix, *The Lord Keeps Me—Mark:16*. The gauze was off the arm. Ming opened the manual.

"Okay, so down here, and then across." She pointed with the blunt edge of the blade.

"Mark. From the Bible, right?" said Sri.

"It's one of the four books in the second half," said Chen.

"What is that part?"

"Umm. I don't know. The overview is simple: Jesus died on the cross to save us, rose from the dead after three days. As for Mark 16..."

"It must mean something," said Sri.

"I'll look it up for you," said Chen.

"Why don't we cut around?" Sri's small finger traced along one arm of the cross.

The cross expanded to curve across each side of the arm in its faded blue wrought ironwork.

"The manual shows," Ming said, "to cut here."

"It is a shame," said Chen, "to cut this apart." The manual's illustration advised an incision directly over the tattooed arm.

"We can easily cut around." Sri spun his scalpel in the fingers of one hand, which he often did until someone reminded him, or he remembered, that it was not a pen.

"What are you going to do," said Ming, "save this?"

"It's bad luck," said Sri. "Cut around here." He traced around the ornate heart with the handle of his scalpel.

"It's a nice cross," agreed Chen.

"You guys." Ming didn't look up. She traced the lines on the arm. "It's not going to work. Don't you want to see the bicipital groove?"

"You should respect a man's symbols," said Sri. "My mother told me that. Look at his arm. These are his symbols."

"Don't your people burn the corpses, anyhow?" said Ming, grabbing the tattooed arm.

"He's not my people."

"Let's get on with it."

"But that's not the point," said Sri.

"So what's the point? You afraid of lightning bolts?"

"I'm not afraid of you." He twirled the scalpel nervously, met Ming's stare.

"Why don't you cut around," said Chen, breaking their locked eyes. "Then dissect the subcutaneous layer? It'll be the same."

* * *

Dr. Harrison was an origami man. In his room of eight tables, they first learned how to make paper boats.

"Let me show you how to tuck in the corners so that it'll be tight and waterproof," *he said. Each day in the lab, after dissection, came the origami. "All right my friends, I hope you've learned well and are ready to set your knowledge free." Each day, every student had to select a page from the lab manual, cut it out carefully at the spiral binding, and fold it into that day's paper figure. After the boats came paper frogs. Then the paper balls that you needed to blow into. They were advised to choose a clean page. They learned that it was easy to make swans from knowing a boat, if you had the trick.*

"If you want to take more than one page out of your manual, you may do so," *he said, "Of course, I may test you from that page. Only anatomy manual origami is allowed." It was known that you should make notes before taking out a page. You had to take out at least one page.*

The swans were hung over the cadavers with twine, and if you forgot something you could look up and see if it was printed on the wing of a twirling swan.

* * *

Halfway through the semester, the days were ending earlier. The sky turned blood to black in the late afternoon. Sri and Chen came in from a dinner break—veggie dogs. Ming didn't take breaks, instead munched granola bars in the museum section of the basement. They had to stay late because it was the evening before the anatomy midterm. Most of the class was still in the basement, and the two of them found Ming rummaging through the bags of body parts, searching. She explained the situation to them, frustrated but not apologetic.

"What do you mean you lost the right side of the head?" Chen asked quietly.

"No, I didn't exactly lose it. It's simply not where I left it," said Ming.

"You put it in the head bag?" said Sri.

"Anyway, we've got the left side. We can look at someone else's right."

"The exam's tomorrow," said Chen. The right and left halves of the head had been dissected differently, and the parts needed from the right had been removed from the left.

"Just think for a second. Are you sure you left it here?" said Sri, fingering the bag which contained the left half of the head.

"I'm sure. I covered it. I sprayed it. It was right here."

"You're always in such a rush," said Sri. "Maybe if you slowed down. You know how long I spent dissecting those cranial nerves?"

"I bet someone took it," said Ming.

Sri replied, "Right. Make up a story. You were looking at it, so it was your responsibility to put it back. With the rest of Murphy."

"Who made you boss? He's not a Murphy," said Ming. "Probably someone borrowed it—it'll turn up."

"You lost the head," Sri whispered, leaning forward and looking at Ming, "and I named him Murphy."

"It's only half. And I did not lose it. I left it right here. It's not where I left it. That's not 'losing' it."

"Obviously you don't care," said Sri.

"Just study it from the manual."

"I made the cranial nerve page into a swan," said Chen. He rested his latex hands on the table.

Ming said, "Should have chosen a different page."

* * *

At two in the morning, only Sri and Chen were in the lab sitting over the borrowed right half of a head. All the other tables were covered in sheets, and sprayed in the fresh pungency of formalin.

"You know she won't apologise, but you probably should," said Chen.

"Why?"

"Because we've still got the pelvis and legs to do. It'll be better if you make peace."

"This is very bad."

"Sure you guys are upset, so just smooth it out."

"Not just her. Losing half his head is bad. And why did she insist we had to cut through Murphy's cross and heart?"

"She follows the book, Sri. She reads it, she does it."

"My mother told me you should respect a man's symbols. We should have cut around the cross. Did you look up that Mark thing?"

"Sorry, I forgot. What was it again?"

"Mark 16."

"I'll check it for you. Did your mother say anything about losing half a head?"

"Never came up."

They looked down at the open half-head which they had only been able to study after midnight when another group had finished. Ming had decided to study from the anatomy atlas.

"Ready for tomorrow?"

"Ready as ever, I guess," said Sri.

"I guess we're done here. Hungry?"

"Kind of. I need something filling to help me sleep."

"Let's go."

In the night, walking under blowing elms, they smelled themselves more clearly, their skin sticky in the armpits and elbows. In the creases of their hands. In the washroom of Nona's, while the round lady heated their calzones, Chen washed his face with his hands, and the more he washed the more that odor seeped from between his fingers and the nails. Under the low wattage light, he used the tepid water and hard soap to wash his hands raw.

* * *

After the midterm, Sri went to Dean Cortina and asked to switch to a different group.

He said, "One of my partners is great but I have a communication problem with my other colleague."

"The course is almost over, and we can't change the groups. I'm glad you said colleague because that means you think like a professional. Take this as your first professional challenge," said Cortina. "I remember my anatomy group and I don't want to tell you how many years ago." She sat back in her big chair. "We had a communication problem. Men are odd about penises. They don't want to talk about them but they secretly believe them to be very important, perhaps sacred. So now we got to the penis on our cadaver, and the men wanted to skip it. 'We'll look at the book,' they said. 'No way,' I said, 'we need to see the inside of the penis.' Corpus spongiosum, all that jazz. Besides, the poor guy's body was lying there. A big man, powerful, and it would have been a shame just to let it go to waste. What did we do? We talked. We talked like professionals, and I saw that it was this one guy's turn to dissect, and there was no way that this man was going to cut up a penis. So I said, 'What if I do it?' and I did it, and I think we all understood the issue better. Does that help?" Sri couldn't think of anything to say. He thanked Dean Cortina and left her office.

* * *

When they got to the penis, there was no problem or hesitation. It was Ming's turn to cut, and she went right through it with one long arc of the scalpel, so that was all there was to it. She said,

"You guys okay?"

"Sure," said Chen.

"Someone want the testicles?"

Both Chen and Sri declined politely, and so Ming did the rest of that day's dissection—producing a fine display of the epididymis and the spermatic ducts. Late after the final exam, some of the class were still at the upstairs patio bar of 'The Paradise.' Many of Harrison's group were there, setting liquor-doused paper napkin swans alight in blue bursts. It was their private party, and they were trying to stay warm beneath the stars, helped by flame-ringed overhead heaters which smelled like burp. Someone had vomited on the toilet seat in the men's rooms and then had just closed the stall door, so now there were lineups for both the male and female washrooms. Others sat in booths, and in a far corner Sri had just bought Ming a vodka tonic. He was feeling good about himself for having bought the drink and she was feeling big about herself for accepting it.

She said, "Guess what, I found the right side of head. It was in the bag with the omentum." Ming couldn't remember exactly how she got it in there, but of course no one had looked at the omentum before the midterm and so she recently found it when she was studying for the final, while looking for a kidney. Then she remembered she must have put it there. A moment of inattention, she said.

"Where is it now?" said Sri.

"Still there."

"With the omentum?" The omentum attached all the intestines into a fan-shaped sheet. "Why didn't you put it with the head?"

"I don't know. The bag wasn't handy, I guess."

"You guess. So you just left it with all the guts and everything," said Sri. "I'll have to go get it."

"What?"

"I'm gonna go get it," he shouted. No one turned to look, in the way that drunk people do not notice each other as being out of the ordinary.

"You're all screwed up," said Ming quietly, "do you dream about your Murphy?"

"Me? You should have nightmares, the way you treat him."

"Hello? Dead? Remember? I don't have dreams, because I don't have hang-ups about the stupid corpse."

"You—"

"You what?" said Ming, "You don't like that? Corpse? Piece of Murphy meat?"

"You're just such a—"

"Just say it. What am I? You want to say it. Call me a name, go ahead and relieve your repressed little self. Say it."

"No. Let's just stop. No."

"Go for it, pick a name. Bitch? Witch? Name your name."

"I didn't say anything, you're picking the words now."

"You're such a wimp, I have to call myself names just to clarify what you think of me," said Ming.

Chen was pushing sideways through the falling dancers. He arrived in time to hear Ming say to Sri, "Just fuck off. See, I can say what I think." She stalked off, weaving across the floor.

"You guys," said Chen to both of them but now just Sri.

"It was better for a minute. Believe it or not. I bought her a drink. Then she told me she found the head. Okay, but she didn't put it back! I can't believe she just misplaced it like that, like it doesn't matter, and then she didn't even put it with the other half? It's with the omentum."

"How many have you had?"

"My mother told me that alcohol can build and then burn bridges between people."

"Your mother."

"Well, it's done now. I'm gonna go get the head."

"Aw... Sri."

"I gotta get it, put it back on."

"Whaddaya mean, come on, wait—"

Already walking away, "I gotta go—"

"Hey wait." Chen, still holding his bottle, went down the stairs after his friend.

* * *

In the anatomy lab, Chen summarised the story.

He said, "Yeah, I looked it up for you. Mark 16: So after Jesus is crucified the women go to wash and prepare Jesus' body with spices. On the road they realise they won't be able to move this huge stone door in front of the tomb. But when they get there, surprise! The door is open and there's no corpse. *Don't be scared,* says the shining angel who's there. *Jesus has risen so tell the disciples that he will comfort and lead them.* The women are scared. Jesus appears to Mary. She tells people about seeing him, but they think she's crazy, so he has to keep on showing himself to people until they're convinced. Anyhow, Jesus says that things are really going well, and all his people will do incredible wonderful things, and be protected even from drinking poison. He says that his followers will be healers by putting their hands on people. Then he goes to heaven to sit with God." Chen put down his beer next to Murphy.

"Is that really what it says?" said Sri.

"Roughly. I looked it up, but I am paraphrasing."

"It's good."

"You still want to put the head back on," said Chen.

"Yeah."

They unwrapped the stump neck, and took the left side of the head from inside the belly where they had left it to be moist. They found the right side in the omentum bag, and the right and left didn't match up exactly anymore because of the dissection. They put the two pieces on top, and Chen could see that Sri wasn't happy, so he wrapped some gauze around the neck to hold things in place.

"He's a bit dry."

"Needs a drink. Bless you, Murphy." Instead of taking the formalin spray bottle, Sri took the rest of Chen's beer, and poured it gently and slowly from the lips to the open belly.

"You don't drink, do you?" said Chen.

"Not usually."

"You have a knack for it."

"Why do you think Murphy chose Mark 16?" Sri closed his eyes. "It's a weird passage. Is that the end of the Jesus story?"

"I guess that a pilot would have figured there wouldn't be a body left for anyone. Nothing left for his girlfriend, or mother. Maybe Mark 16 made him feel better about that."

"He was wrong," said Sri, bowing his head, his arms stretched to the shining table now dull with the running of liquid. Beer dripped into the bucket between Murphy's feet. "He's here for us."

Sri wound a strip of yellowed fabric up the neck, pulled it tight over the chin so it wouldn't bunch, then softly over the eyes, and the coldness of the eyelids vanished in the swath of cloth. Murphy's hair had continued to grow for a little while after being shaved, and Chen held up the stubbled head for Sri to work. Sri wound the fabric around the top of the skull, and tied it onto itself snugly with a slipless knot under the angle of the jaw. Sri stood back, and saw where the tip of the right ear protruded. He tugged gently at a fold of cotton, and settled it around the ear, where it would stay.

Source: From "Take all of Murphy" reprinted from Bloodletting and miraculous cures *by Vincent Lam.*

Copyright © 2005 by Vincent Lam. Reprinted by permission from Doubleday Canada.

Model APA citation

Lam, V. (2005). Take all of Murphy. In *Bloodletting and miraculous cures* (pp. 31–53). Toronto, Canada: Doubleday Canada.

Discussion Questions:

1. The three students, Ming, Sri and Chen, all have distinct characteristics. Describe their various personalities.

2. The lab partners disagree several times throughout the story. What things create conflict amongst them?

3. Tension between Ming and Sri escalates in the story. What do you think is at the root of this discord?

4. Think of the challenges and rewards you have had working in groups, whether that be for school projects or work-related tasks. Compare your group experience(s) with Sri, Chen, and Ming's experience of being partnered in the dissection lab.

5. What is the subtext of Dean Cortina's story on p. 198. In other words, what wisdom or advice does the Dean impart to Sri?

6. Why do you think Sri wants to name the cadaver and Ming does not? What about Chen? What is his stance? How do you think you would respond if you were in the same situation?

7. What ethical dilemmas are at play in the story? For example, what do the discussions of whether to name the cadaver, cut through the crucifix tattoo, or restore the detached head suggest about personal and professional distance?

8. Lam is careful to include details of the changing season, how the early days of autumn at the story's opening give way to shorter and darker days by the story's end. What impact do these seasonal descriptions have? And, how do they relate to the larger issues and themes explored in "Take All of Murphy"?

9. Describe Murphy's tattoos. What story do these tattoos tell, in regards both to Murphy's life and to the personalities of the three medical students?

10. Read the last paragraph of the story carefully. Why does the story end this way? Is anything resolved, or does the ending create more ambiguity and complexity?

11. Why do you think Lam titled his story "Take All of Murphy"?

12. What do you think Vincent Lam intended to impart to his readers about the world of medicine in "Take All of Murphy"? Do you think he is successful?

13. What aspects of this story relate to your chosen health profession? Find as many connections as you can.

OTHER STORIES FOR YOUR CONSIDERATION

• "Cathedral," by Raymond Carver

A man initially hostile toward a blind man is transformed by his interaction with him.

Themes: blindness, disability, ignorance, discrimination

Model APA citation

Carver, R. (2008). Cathedral. In R. S. Gwynn & W. Campbell (Eds.), *Fiction: A pocket anthology* (2nd Can. ed., pp. 238–252). Toronto, Canada: Pearson. (Original work published 1983)

• "The Model," by Bernard Malamud

An aging man tries to ease his loneliness and recapture his youth by painting a young model.

Themes: aging, loneliness, alienation, reminiscence

Model APA citation

Malamud, B. (1995). The model. In S. Marcus (Ed.), *A world of fiction: Twenty timeless short stories* (pp. 145–149). New York, NY: Addison-Wesley. (Original work published 1983)

- "The Yellow Wallpaper," by Charlotte Perkins Gilman

A misunderstood woman mentally "unravels" in 19th century America.

Themes: mental illness, misdiagnosis, depression, confinement, insanity, repression

Model APA citation

Gilman, C. P. (2005). The yellow wallpaper. In R. S. Gwynn (Ed.), *Fiction: A pocket anthology* (4th ed., pp. 88–103). New York, NY: Pearson. (Original work published 1892)

- "Miss Brill," by Katherine Mansfield

A weekly ritual forces an aging woman to confront the harsh reality of her age and situation.

Themes: aging, ageism, isolation, reminiscence

Model APA citation

Mansfield, K. (2008). Miss Brill. In R. S. Gwynn & W. Campbell (Eds.), *Fiction: A pocket anthology* (2nd Can. ed., pp. 119–123). Toronto, Canada: Pearson. (Original work published 1922)

- "The Use of Force," by William Carlos Williams

A power struggle ensues between a doctor and his child patient as he tries to diagnose her.

Themes: doctor–patient relationships, empathy, control

Model APA citation

Williams, W. C. (1952). The use of force. Retrieved from http://www.classicshorts.com/stories/force.html (Reprinted from *An approach to literature*, pp. 31–33)

TRY IT YOURSELF

Using the previous model APA citations as a guide, for each of the remaining stories create your own APA reference page citation. Make sure to follow all APA rules regarding punctuation, capitalization, and italics. You will have to go to the library or use the Internet to locate the required information for each entry. Answers will vary so check with your instructor.

- "A Face of Stone," by William Carlos Williams

A doctor initially annoyed by two of his immigrant patients learns valuable lessons about judgment, courage, and survival.

Themes: doctor–patient relationships, prejudice, medical stress

Reference

_____

_____

- "The Bear Came Over the Mountain," by Alice Munro

Alzheimer's disease impacts the life of a long-time married couple when the woman has to be institutionalized.

Themes: dementia, memory, loss, regret, reminiscence, fidelity, guilt, nursing homes

Reference

_____

_____

- "God Is Not a Fish Inspector," by W. D. Valgaardson

A feisty elderly man hangs onto his pride and dignity despite various forces that work against him.

Themes: aging, inheritance, pride, reminiscence, nursing homes

Reference

_____

_____

POEMS TO EXAMINE AND EXPLORE

The following two poems, "Do Not Go Gentle into That Good Night," (1952) by Dylan Thomas, and "The Last Words of My English Grandmother," (1924) by William Carlos Williams, both explore the themes of death and dying. Thomas's poem is a plea from a son to his dying father to fight against his inevitable death, while Williams's poem portrays an elderly woman's fear and stubbornness as she is taken to the hospital in an ambulance. Read each poem carefully, and then work in small groups to discuss the questions that follow each reading.

DO NOT GO GENTLE INTO THAT GOOD NIGHT
by Dylan Thomas

Do not go gentle into that good night,
Old age should burn and rage at close of day;
Rage, rage against the dying of the light.

Though wise men at their end know dark is right,
Because their words had forked no lightning they
Do not go gentle into that good night.

Good men, the last wave by, crying how bright
Their frail deeds might have danced in a green bay,
Rage, rage against the dying of the light.

Wild men who caught and sang the sun in flight,
And learn, too late, they grieved it on its way,
Do not go gentle into that good night.

Grave men, near death, who see with blinding sight
Blind eyes could blaze like meteors and be gay,
Rage, rage against the dying of the light.

And you, my father, there on the sad height,
Curse, bless me now with your fierce tears, I pray.
Do not go gentle into that good night.
Rage, rage against the dying of the light.

Source: From THE POEMS OF DYLAN THOMAS, *by Dylan Thomas. Copyright © 1952 by Dylan Thomas. Reprinted by permission of New Directions Publishing Corp.*

Model APA citation

Thomas, D. (2009). Do not go gentle into that good night. In R. S. Gwynn (Ed.), *Literature: A pocket anthology* (4th ed., p. 643). New York, NY: Pearson. (Original work published 1952)

Discussion Questions:

1. What repeated words and phrases do you notice in this poem? Make a list. Why do you think the poet chooses to repeat these words and phrases?

2. The word *death* appears only once in this poem. What are some of the indirect ways that the poet refers to death? Why do you think he chooses these phrases, rather than write about death directly?

3. Why do you think the speaker does not want his father to accept his death? Why does he ask him to fight? Would you ask the same of a loved one? Why or why not?

THE LAST WORDS OF MY ENGLISH GRANDMOTHER
by William Carlos Williams

There were some dirty plates
and a glass of milk
beside her small table
near the rank, dishevelled bed—

Wrinkled and nearly blind
she lay and snored
rousing with anger in her tones
to cry for food,

Gimme something to eat—
They're starving me—
I'm all right I won't go
to the hospital. No, no, no

you can do as you please.
She smiled, Yes
you do what you please first
then I can do what I please—

Oh, oh, oh! she cried
as the ambulance men lifted
her to the stretcher—
Is this what you call

making me comfortable?
By now her mind was clear—
Oh you think you're smart
you young people,

she said, but I'll tell you
you don't know anything.
Then we started.
On the way

we passed a long row
of elms. She looked at them
awhile out of
the ambulance window and said,

What are all those
fuzzy-looking things out there?
Trees? Well, I'm tired
of them and rolled her head away.

Source: From THE COLLECTED POEMS: VOLUME I, 1909–1939, *by William Carlos Williams. Copyright © 1938 by New Directions Publishing Corp.*

Model APA citation

Williams, W. C. (1941). The last words of my English grandmother. Retrieved from http://www.americanpoems.com/poets/williams/9079

Discussion Questions:

1. What words would you use to describe the poet's grandmother's attitude and behaviour? Why do you think she behaves this way?

2. She says that she doesn't want to go to the hospital; why is she taken there in spite of her protests?

3. Have you experienced the aging, dementia, and/or death of a loved one? How did that person cope with the process?

4. What are the grandmother's last words? What do you think she means by them? What can readers learn from them?

OTHER POEMS FOR YOUR CONSIDERATION

• "When I have fears," by John Keats

Model APA citation

Keats, J. (2006). When I have fears. In J. S. Scott, R. E. Jones, & R. Bowers (Eds.), *The Harbrace anthology of literature* (4th ed., p. 145). Toronto, Canada: Nelson. (Original work published 1848)

- "King Lear in Respite Care," by Margaret Atwood

Model APA citation

Atwood, M. (1995). King Lear in respite care. Retrieved from http://www.poetryarchive.org/poetryarchive/singlePoem.do?poemId=99 (Reprinted from *Selected poems*, by Margaret Atwood, 1976, New York, NY: Houghton Mifflin)

TRY IT YOURSELF

Using the previous model APA citations as a guide, for each of the remaining poems create your own APA reference page citation. Make sure to follow all APA rules regarding punctuation, capitalization, and italics. You will have to go to the library or use the Internet to locate the required information for each entry. As answers will vary, check with your instructor.

- "Waking in the Blue," by Robert Lowell

Reference

- "Tubes," by Donald Hall

Reference

- "In the Operating Room," by Alden Nowlan

Reference

FILMS TO WATCH AND INTERPRET

The following ten films are thematically related to health care. Your instructor may choose to show one or more in class, or you may opt to view some of them on your own or with classmates. Each film raises complex ethical issues that provide many points for you to discuss. For example, what ethical issues are involved in the Fitzgeralds' decision to engineer a child to be a genetic match and donor for their first child, who has leukemia, in *My Sister's Keeper*? Or in John Nash's decision to stop taking his antipsychotic medication in *A Beautiful Mind*? Many of these films portray exemplary health care professionals, such as the title character in *Patch Adams* or Nurse Susie Monahan in *Wit*, while many others show health care professionals behaving unprofessionally or unethically, such as Nurse Ratched in *One Flew Over the Cuckoo's Nest* or Frank Pierce in *Bringing Out the Dead*. While watching these films, ask yourself how you would behave—as a patient, as a family member, as a health professional—in the situations depicted.

- *A Beautiful Mind* (2001)

This Academy Award-winning film is based on the life of Nobel Prize-winning mathematician John Nash, who suffered from paranoid schizophrenia. As Nash witnesses the pain that his condition brings to his wife and friends, he also struggles with the decision to control his delusions through medication, knowing that it would impede his genius for mathematics, as well as his ability to connect emotionally to his wife.

Themes: schizophrenia, medication, delusions, genius, psychosis, paranoia

Model APA citation

Howard, R. (Director). (2002). *A beautiful mind* [Motion picture]. United States: Universal Pictures.

- *Bringing Out the Dead* (1999)

Frank Pierce is a paramedic on the night shift in New York City, who is beginning to feel powerless to save lives. Collapsing under the burden of other people's pain and suffering, and unable to sleep, he repeatedly attempts to get fired.

Themes: paramedics, working with others, loss of patients, job burnout

Model APA citation

Scorsese, M. (Director). (1999). *Bringing out the dead* [Motion picture]. United States: De Fina-Cappa.

- *God Said "Ha!"* (1998)

In a filmed monologue, comedian Julia Sweeney tells of caring for her brother Mike during the year between his cancer diagnosis and his death. First Mike and then her parents move in with her, and they use humour to cope with a tragic situation.

Themes: cancer, medical treatments, family support, humour, health insurance

Model APA citation

Sweeney, J. (Director). (1998). *God said "ha!"* [Motion picture]. United States: Oh Brother Productions Inc.

Using the previous model APA citations as a guide, for each of the remaining films create your own APA reference page citation. Make sure to follow all APA rules regarding punctuation, capitalization and italics. You will have to go to the library or use the Internet to locate the required information for each entry. As answers will vary, check with your instructor.

- *My Sister's Keeper* (2009)

This film, based on the book by Jodi Picoult, centres around a family trying to do everything they can to save their daughter from leukemia, including having a child by in vitro fertilization in order to supply genetic material to their dying daughter. The second daughter eventually rebels from her role as genetic donor and attempts to sue her parents.

Themes: bioethics, leukemia, autonomy, right to life, organ donation

Reference

- *Patch Adams* (1998)

This film is based on the true story of Hunter Adams, a man who is inspired to be a doctor for all the right reasons. His unusual approach to doctoring and healing draws both praise and criticism.

Themes: eccentricity, alternative healing methods, depression, doctor–patient relationships, rebellion, malpractice

Reference

- *Sicko* (2007)

The acclaimed documentary filmmaker Michael Moore sheds light on some of the failings of American health care by comparing it to systems in Canada, France, and Britain. Moore's documentary exposes some surprising injustices.

Themes: public health care, private health care, health insurance, quality of care, cost of care

Reference

- *Vera Drake* (2004)

Vera Drake is a character who takes medicine into her own hands in 1950s England by conducting abortions on women despite not being qualified to do so. Her illegal doctoring is eventually exposed and consequences follow.

Themes: abortion, ethics, nursing, malpractice

Reference

_____

_____

- *Wit* (2001)

This film, based on the Pulitzer Prize-winning play by Margaret Edson, follows English professor Vivian Bearing as she undergoes experimental treatments for ovarian cancer. Vivian attempts to maintain her dignity and humanity as she realizes that her doctors see her as a research subject rather than a human being.

Themes: death and dying, doctor–patient relationships, nursing, experimental treatments, re-evaluation of values

Reference

_____

_____

- *50/50* (2011)

Adam Learner has a rare form of cancer. Throughout the treatment process, he learns much about life, illness and coping all while professional boundaries between him and his counsellor become blurred. The movie depicts the roller coaster ride of illness and showcases the unpredictability of disease.

Themes: cancer, chemotherapy, doctor-patient relationships, Alzheimer's disease, coping, unpredictability of illness

Reference

_____

_____

CHAPTER LINKS FOR FURTHER EXPLORATION

• Arts Health Network (http://artshealthnetwork.ca)

The Arts Health Network (Canada) attempts to foster connections between health and the arts in the belief that the arts impact health and well-being. The site has a comprehensive Resource section which provides specific links to topical material, including newsletters and journal articles.

• The National Film Board of Canada (http://www.nfb.ca)

The National Film Board of Canada's website lists numerous films (documentary and commercial) on topics related to health and medicine. Health film topics are diverse and include coping with illness and dying and medical perspectives.

• Goodreads (http://www.goodreads.com/shelf/show/mental-illness)

Novels that explore mental illness are listed here. The site's list of novels that incorporate this theme is vast and includes both classic and modern titles. Summaries of each novel are provided; additionally, many books are commented on and rated by readers.

INDEX